EAST RIDING YESTERDAY

EAST RIDING YESTERDAY

MAVE & BEN CHAPMAN

Smith
Settle

First published in 2002 by
Smith Settle Ltd
Ilkley Road
Otley
West Yorkshire
LS21 3JP

ISBN Paperback 1 85825 172 9
Hardback 1 85825 173 7

British Library Cataloguing-in-Publication data:
A catalogue record for this book is available from the British Library.

Set in Monotype Bembo

Designed, printed and bound by
SMITH SETTLE
Ilkley Road, Otley, West Yorkshire LS21 3JP

Contents

MAVE CHAPMAN, 1933–1998

This East Riding volume is dedicated to my late wife Mave, it being the last project we worked upon as a team, though much of the research was done by her. I hope this book will serve as a memorial to a loving wife, soulmate and best friend.

Acknowledgements

WE WOULD LIKE TO express our grateful thanks to Muriel Kirk and her father the late Floyd Kirk for their help and support with information about the Methodist Church, and also for the happy hours which were spent with Floyd who related to us many stories of life in Holderness.

To Terry Kendall who proudly told us numerous stories of his grandfather's exploits, and to Joy and Jim Drewery for their interest and loan of a photograph of Robert Drewery.

Thanks to Molly Lawton for patiently answering our questions and being helpful on a number of occasions.

Scarborough and Withernsea libraries have both been very helpful with research material, as have the staff of the local history library in Hull, and Ann Willey of Hull Reference Library.

Thanks also to all the many people we have spoken to who have told us about life in the early part of the twentieth century, and passed on stories of their parents and grandparents. Without the co-operation of these people who have been so generous with their time, we would not have been able to portray the atmosphere of life before the Second World War.

A special vote of thanks to James Maxwell of Easington for sharing with us his encyclopaedic knowledge of his village, and Wayne Wolton of Withernsea for his valuable advice and help with photography.

Reasonable attempts have been made to trace all owners of copyright where applicable, but we would be glad to hear, via the publishers, from anyone who thinks they may have been overlooked.

Mave and Ben Chapman
Withernsea, July 2001

Introduction

O N THE 1st April 1996, Humberside County Council ceased to exist. Since its inception in 1974, the name Humberside had proved controversial, especially amongst many of the people living in the old East Riding of Yorkshire.

This book is a celebration motivated by the return of the name East Yorkshire to the statute books, which for the sake of this volume is based loosely on popular definition rather than geographical location. The East Riding to many holidaymakers includes Scarborough as well as the towns of Filey and Bridlington, each of which is represented here.

The landscape of East Yorkshire may not be as dramatic as other parts of the county, being, with the exception of the Wolds, mainly flat. This we believe adds to its charm in the eyes of many who perceive a certain tranquil beauty in its rural vistas.

We have included pictures covering the agricultural areas of the Wolds, and such historic places as Howden and Selby. The city of Kingston-upon-Hull naturally features to a large extent, being the major conurbation in the area. A publication entitled *A Descriptive Account of Modern Hull* was produced in 1892. It informed its readers that 'Hull, or more accurately, Kingston Upon Hull, is in many senses, one of the most remarkable towns to be met in the United Kingdom. Its annals are replete with historic interest, and from medieval times downward bear ample witness to the part it has played in the evolution of our national greatness.'

We have illustrated the book with a high proportion of picture postcards, but we have also included a number of old photographs from our extensive collection, in order to present some of the remarkable people of the area, their lifestyle, and some of the events which have influenced their day-to-day existence such as floods and other disasters. Our aim has been to illustrate as fully as possible the many facets of the daily lives of East Yorkshire folk in a bygone age, roughly from 1890 to 1950. We have included in our selection people at work and play, places of interest not normally seen, local worthies and some of the events which illustrate the more serious side of life.

The personalities we have chosen cannot be said, with a few exceptions, to have achieved national fame, but were well known to our forbears. Most of the anecdotes we have related about these people have a firm basis in truth but we believe one or two are possibly apocryphal, and we leave the reader to form their own opinions.

Many of the pictures are previously unpublished, and it is hoped that they may evoke happy memories in older readers, and present the younger reader with a picture of a now-vanished way of life.

People and Personalities

THE *Oxford English Dictionary* defines personality as 'distinctive personal character'. This suggests a person who has some individual trait such as charm, charisma, intelligence or perhaps a highly-developed sense of purpose which singles him or her out from mainstream society and sets them apart in some remarkable way. Society has labelled many of these individuals as 'eccentrics', usually because it was not easy to define an often whimsical character.

No two people are exactly alike in personality, although most of us fit somewhere into the schemes devised by the psychologist. Fortunately life has been enriched by the individuals who for various reasons cannot be so easily defined. A classic example is the person who has become excessively self-reliant, possible as a result of being the only surviving member of a family at an early age, perhaps as a result of a disaster or more likely due to the shorter life expectancy of our forbears. In many cases these individuals won the respect and admiration of their contemporaries by their efforts to overcome their disadvantages, a situation which often worked to the benefit of the community. Then there were those who had a highly developed sense of service to others and thereby gained the regard of their fellow man.

People have been motivated in a diversity of ways to provide for themselves, one of the more remarkable of these being the street entertainer. Some have been talented above the normally accepted concept in various fields and as such have left their mark on society. The people we have chosen to portray have all shown characteristics which have recommended them in some way as notable. Their fame varies. Some have only been noteworthy in their own localities, others have achieved a modicum of national acclaim, but all have followed a way of life which has singled them out as remarkable.

Today society does not allow the kind of individuality which was the hallmark of the 'local character'. In spite of the so-called liberated age, there is a compulsion to conform to what is designated as a 'normal lifestyle'. Quite what is meant by this is inexplicable, but consequently some of the people we describe would not have been allowed to live their often useful lives and make their contribution to the community, in the way they did in a slower-paced, more tolerant age.

It is fortunate that there are still elderly people who can relate anecdotes and give reliable facts which can be recorded, and thereby, even if only in a small way, the lives of some of these personalities can be written down before it is too late.

We have chosen the people who we think best represent the East Riding, and there are obviously many who are still well-remembered that we have not been able to include. We have tried to choose the people who have not become world famous and extensively documented, in the hope of offering new interest and an insight into life in the region around a century ago.

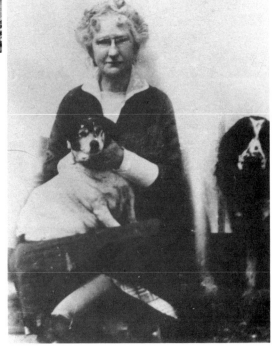

Edith Louisa Cavell (1865–1915) was a British nurse who was shot by the Germans for helping soldiers to escape from Belgium. She was matron of the Birkendael Medical Institute, Brussels, and is said to have helped more than 200 wounded English, French and Belgian soldiers to escape to the Dutch frontier. She was executed on the 12th October 1915.

Edith was a clergyman's daughter and had a younger sister, Florence Mary Scott Cavell *(see picture)*. Florence also became a nurse and was the matron of the convalescent home and hospital at Withernsea from 1914 to 1945. There seems to be some doubt as to her exact date of birth, as it is not recorded on her gravestone in St Nicholas's churchyard in Withernsea, but which record that she died on the 2nd June 1950. As Edith attained national fame for her outstanding courage and bravery, so Florence became a well-respected member of the local community. Many townspeople still have anecdotes to relate of their encounters with Matron Cavell. One lady mentioned that she made her rounds in the evening for many years with a lamp which she described as 'like Florence Nightingale'.

Annie Croft was born at Skirlaugh on the 17th August 1896. Her parents were Michael and Emma (*née* Harlan) Croft. Her earliest stage triumph was when she entered a singing competition at the age of six at the Thornton Street Band of Hope in Hull, winning third prize. The choirmaster of the Band of Hope, Mr Watson Boyes, was so impressed with Annie's performance that he gave her a place in the choir and personally supervised her training. She took musical examinations under the tutelage of Madame Sharrah at Hull School of Music.

Having organised a children's concert at the age of ten, she became a teacher and taught the children, many of whom were her friends, after school. Her concerts were soon a huge success. (The group photograph shows Annie centre back with large hat with some of her young pupils.) Her next triumph was the part of Yum Yum in the *Mikado*, presented by the Hull Operatic Society, and from then on she was in great demand throughout Yorkshire. At the age of thirteen she appeared for two months in Bridlington under the name of Melba Drew, having been given a special permit to work.

Annie made her first London appearance at the Shaftesbury Theatre on the 27th August 1914, succeeding Cicely Courtneidge as Phylis in *The Cinema Star*. In 1915 she married Reginald Hanson Sharland at St Stephen's Church in Hull. Sadly this marriage was dissolved in 1931 after Reginald went to live in Los Angeles in 1929.

In 1931 she was interviewed by a reporter from the *Hull Times* who described her as 'actress, producer, composer, librettist and public speaker'. Annie really made the top of her profession in the 1930s and had her name in lights in the West End on more than one occasion. Her recreations were given in *Who's Who in the Theatre* at this period as motoring and fishing.

In 1867 a boy who was named Andie Taylor was born. Nothing appears to have been recorded about his parents and young Andie was brought up in an orphanage, suggesting that there was possibly personal tragedy in his early life. He later changed his name to Andie Caine, and was to become a much-loved and respected citizen of Filey.

Again there is some doubt about the date when he first became an entertainer on Filey beach, but the generally held view comes down in favour of 1894. He always claimed that he came to Filey after a season or two at Scarborough and Bridlington with Will Catlin, which would place it nearer to the turn of the century.

Andie's first appearance was as a busker with George Fisher. They dressed in Pierrot costumes and, whilst Andie strummed a banjo, George accompanied him on the strill (portable harmonium). They delighted their audiences with good strong tenor renditions of such songs of the period as *Just a Bit of String* and *Said the Bell on Nellie's Hat*. They were soon joined by Teddy Myles, a Leeds comedian, and being too poor to have digs, they slept on the beach. There was however some unpleasantness when fishermen, who considered them a nuisance, emptied fish heads and other offal on their pitch. Differences were soon resolved when Andie pointed out to them that the crowds they attracted all spent money and probably ate fish. This proved a turning point for Andie: he prospered, added to his troupe and married. His new bride and her sister joined the troupe as a double act. They later had two children who were affectionately known as Sonny and Girlie.

In 1913, Andie opened the first cinema in Filey in what was known as the Grand Hall in Union Street, where Andie as Father Christmas would hand out gifts to all the children. He always organised a number of shows for children, perhaps due to his experiences as an orphan. Throughout the First World War the troupe continued to perform — Andie, now in his late forties, was not eligible for active service.

Andie eventually acquired the Southdenes Pavilion, which he converted into a theatre, and it is said that some of his shows were visited by royalty which included the Mountbatten family, hence his title 'Royal Filey Pierrots'. A regular feature in Filey was Lifeboat Day, with the entire troupe giving impromptu performances all around the town and collecting much-needed funds. Andie continued to prosper, eventually owning a theatre, cinema and two boarding houses. He took an active part in the affairs of Filey Hospital and became a councillor.

Andie Caine passed away on the 22nd November 1941 and was buried in St Oswald's churchyard, Filey. Below the inscription on his gravestone is a small carving of a conical Pierrot hat, a fitting tribute for the orphan who made his way in life through hard graft and consideration for others.

Doctor William Henry Coates (1869–1924) of Bleak House, Patrington, was an outstanding man in many ways. Not only was he a doctor, but a surgeon, barrister, county councillor, and clerk to the parish council. He was responsible for the Kinema being built in Patrington during the First World War. It had a stage, dressing rooms, balcony and a billiard room. The doctor had his own seat in the balcony which was always available for him. (The Kinema later became the village hall.) He was a great benefactor, and entertained the blind and handicapped from Hull at a garden party held at Bleak House every year. He was also an active Liberal and party events were also held at the house. Many are the anecdotes lovingly related about the good doctor by the older generation who remembered him for his humour and kindness, and also as a man with a spirit of adventure who was one of the first in the area to own a motor cycle and a car. This picture was sent by Doctor and Mrs Coates as a Christmas card in 1904.

Mr John Wark Blakeney was a compass adjuster of note in Hull, who commanded very high wages in the early part of the twentieth century — he is reputed at the age of twenty-one to have been earning £2,000 a year. He worked for the second generation of Wilsons, and when he retired through ill health they granted him a generous allowance.

He had a whimsical sense of humour, and in his retirement became a public character. He enjoyed attending political meetings, to the discomfiture of the speakers as he often reduced the gathering to gales of laughter. At election time he was in his element, parading the town in a light suit and hat, wearing a 'buttonhole'. This was so large it would have been more aptly described a bouquet. Mr Blakeney bowed to every lady he met on his walks, and on election day he rode on the top of the trams bowing to the right and to the left like royalty, to the great amusement of the public.

He loved children, and several times a week he bought quantities of ju-jubes from Ripleys confectioners on Spring Bank. These he distributed to any child he met in the street.

It was his habit to go down to the pier wearing his 'buttonhole' and discourse with the travellers from the ferry, setting himself up as a one-man unofficial 'welcoming committee'. Our picture shows 'Hull's popular citizen' wearing his buttonhole and carrying the local newspaper, with the pier in the background.

Brandesburton was once the unlikely home of a group of African pygmies from the Ituri Forest, brought over to England by the celebrated Yorkshire adventurer and big-game hunter Colonel James Jonathan Harrison of Brandesburton Hall. The six diminutive visitors — four men and two women — were Chief Bokane, Princess Quarke, Mufutiminga, Mogonga, Amuriape and Matuka.

The pygmies were very successfully exhibited on the stages of various music halls around the country, their first appearance being at the London Hippodrome on the 5th June 1905. An important diversion from their busy schedule took place in the July, when they attended the twenty-first birthday celebrations of the Princess Victoria at Buckingham Palace. After touring the north of England, they journeyed to Berlin in 1906. Their final public appearance took place on the 16th November 1907 at the Albion Lecture Hall in Hull. The *Hull Daily News* published a short report which said: 'On Sunday they [the pygmies] leave Hull by Wilson liner for Port Said, where they will be joined by Colonel Harrison, who will accompany them to Mombassa, en route to their home'.

During their eighteen-month stay in England, they spent a considerable amount of time at Brandesburton, where, it is said, they lived in a glass conservatory and hunted in the grounds of the hall with home-made bows and arrows. The locals soon accepted the pygmies — they were very intelligent, with an exaggerated sense of fun, were excellent mimics and loved to dance. After their stay they were taken back home by the colonel. All had gained weight, enjoyed their European diet and adapted well to the English mode of dress for the period.

No account of the life in the East Riding would be complete without a mention of Rose Carr. Rose was born on the 2nd December 1843 in North Frodingham, and her name appears in the baptismal register as Rose Ellen Carr, daughter of Mary (*née* Harrison) and John Carr, who is recorded as a grocer and labourer.

She still remains an enigma. There is very little authenticated information concerning her youth, though her illiteracy probably points to a scant if not total lack of education. It is thought that in her early years she was in service at Dringhoe, and it is possible that during this time she was involved in an accident which severely disfigured her face. She was kicked by an animal — either a horse or cow, there seems to be no definite evidence to establish which. The left side of her face was paralysed and badly twisted. Some uncharitable people considered her to be ugly, but others found her appearance frightening. Whilst always being known as Rose Carr, there appear to be various stories and elements which question her gender. Whether she was male or female, the mystery remains, as her sister had her sewn into a shroud when she died.

In her early adult life she was what is now termed a tearaway, known for her drunkenness and fighting (in a most unfeminine manner). By 1872 she had taken over the business in Hornsea of Mr Usher who ran a livery stable. She became a carrier between Hornsea and Beeford, and Hull and Hornsea. The story goes that she always kept a horse on standby for the local doctor. With the advent of the railway, Rose was one of the first sights the holidaymakers had as they disembarked from the train at Hornsea Station, and an impressive sight it was too. She was about five feet six inches (1.7m) tall and weighed nineteen stones (120kg). She could hardly be described as 'at the height of fashion' as her usual mode of dress was a pair of men's boots, a long-skirted black dress with a white apron, and a battered old hat with a flower. She had huge masculine-looking arms and spoke in a gruff voice. She would transport passengers and luggage.

She was highly respected in the area as a hardworking and cheerful person, and as a carrier and livery proprietor she enjoyed a very high reputation. The stories of her strength are legion, and often she performed feats when loading her carrier's cart that left strong men gasping in amazement. The one fact which all accounts agree about Rose was her love for horses and her remarkable skill with the creatures. Other owners often found that her skills with a sick horse could succeed where even a vet failed. In spite of her forbidding appearance, she loved children and was always kind to them. She usually had a few 'spice' (sweets) in her voluminous pockets to hand out.

Rose's other notable activity was her preaching. She had joined the Primitive Methodist church at Beeford early in her life and like all converts she put a great deal of effort into her preaching, and was well known around Hornsea for her vociferous 'hell fire and damnation' sermons. She would not tolerate swearing or what she called cheek, and many a lad was on the receiving end of a 'good clip' for his pains. Rose collected for charities, and one feels that it would have taken courage to resist her. It was her proud boast that, even though she could not read or write, she could count her 'brass'. She had two overriding aversions: the motor car, although there is a postcard of her in a 1903 Panhard; and football, which she referred to as the 'Devil's game'.

Failing health eventually forced Rose to give up her preaching activities. It is said that she knew she was dying, as a few weeks before her death she put her affairs in order. When she died in 1913 it was found that she had willed her not inconsiderable estate to various members of her family.

Although she never travelled far outside her own community, Rose was truly a 'personality'. With the odds against her due to her unfortunate appearance, she won the respect of all who knew her. She had boundless courage to live the life she wanted for herself. At times she must have been very lonely and perhaps longed for love and friendship. This comes to mind when one considers the obvious love and affection she lavished on her horses. It is also apparent that there were residents of Hornsea who because of her kindness, perhaps to them or their children, felt something akin to love for Rose but were reluctant to make an open statement, being unsure of their reception from this remarkable Yorkshirewoman.

Arthur Neville Cooper was born in 1850 in Windsor, and was educated at Christ's Hospital in London. He took his MA degree at Christ's College, Oxford. He served as vicar of St Oswald's Church, Filey, from 1880 until 1935, when he decided reluctantly to retire due to failing eyesight and saddened by the fact that he could no longer read the Bible.

It could be said that his preoccupation with walking really began in Filey. He had always been an enthusiastic pedestrian, but here, with a far-flung parish, it was not at all unusual for him to walk thirty miles (48km) a day. He was an imposing figure, indifferent to weather or time of day as he walked on his rounds, a cheery, affable man with his black hat, knee breeches and knapsack. The canon always carrried a notebook in which he recorded his adventures.

In 1891 he married a local girl, Maude Nicholson, much to the delight of his parishioners. One cannot help feeling that Mrs Cooper, who later bore him two daughters, must have been an exceptionally understanding lady. He became more and more ambitious in his walks, and after Easter services would set off to walk from Filey to Rome, a distance of about 1,000 miles (1,600km), which he managed on foot in six weeks, allowing himself only ten shillings (50p) per day expenses. Other journeys included Filey to Venice (800 miles/1,300km). Hamburg to Paris (500 miles/800km) and Dublin to Limerick (110 miles/180km) — these are but a few. Over the years he visited Scotland and Wales, and went to Budapest, Monte Carlo, Barcelona, Copenhagen, Stockholm and Pompeii; he crossed the Carpathians and also went on a pilgrimage to Lourdes as a pedestrian.

Canon Cooper wrote several books on walking at home and abroad. His church work does not appear to have suffered from his absences. He raised large sums of money for the widows of the forty Filey men lost in the gales of 1880, and also set about finding money for the restoration of St Oswald's and the building of the Church of England infants school.

The proud boast of this remarkable man was that he never needed a physician and attributed his longevity to the beneficial effects of walking. After he retired he continued in reasonable health, and died in his ninety-third year. There is a memorial plaque and a simple gravestone in the sanctuary of St Oswald's Church.

Robert Henry Drewery, or 'Withernsea Bob' as he was better known, was born at Rimswell in 1874. His father was a farmer and the family eventually moved to Southlands Farm at Withernsea.

Bob soon showed an interest in the sea, and by the time he was eleven years old was regularly fishing in the old square-rigged sailing vessels. When he was thirteen he became an apprentice and travelled the world. During this time he served as a member of the first steam trawler to sail from Grimsby. Not long after this voyage he returned to Withernsea, which at this date could reasonably be described as a fishing village. He then worked for a short time before his marriage as a rigger at a shipyard in Hull, where he was highly valued for his skill as a wire splicer.

A newly married man, he soon settled to the trade of inshore fisherman. He had a remarkable knowledge of nature, and was considered locally as a proven weather prophet, making extraordinarily accurate forecasts. His interest in nature led him into taxidermy, and before long he possessed numerous excellent specimens of stuffed fish, birds and animals which he displayed in his 'museum' on Queen Street in Withernsea, opposite the end of Seaside Road.

Tales of Bob are legion and diverse in the extreme, and however incredible they may appear, can all be authenticated. One of the more amazing stories is that he is said to have shot a crow from the flagstaff of the lighthouse with a catapult. He made his own false teeth — after having acquired a full set of beast's teeth and finding them impractical — by melting down some old aluminium saucepans and producing a set of metal teeth.

One of his most celebrated exploits was when he caught a shark in October 1938 which became known locally as the 'Fighting Shark of Hull Fair Fame'. His grandson Terry related the story of how the shark was exhibited at the fair — along with the 'Monster Rats' — as the 'Man-Eating Shark of Witherinsey', and as a teenager Terry cycled to Hull every day to look after 'granddad's shark'. The charge of admission to this wonderful show was a penny. A month later, in November, Bob caught another shark, this time a twenty stone (127kg) monster which he decided should be stuffed for his museum. He was amazed to find a can of ale in the shark's stomach, which he sent with an accompanying photograph to the brewers in London, who expressed its thanks to him.

Not least of Bob's exploits was his association with the Withernsea lifeboat. In those days the boat was rowed manually, and he was the coxwain of the last lifeboat of this kind in Withernsea, the *Docea Chapman*. He was also involved in the building of Withernsea Lighthouse, and proudly claimed to have been the only man who had been under it (digging the foundations), inside it and over it (flying over it in an aeroplane in the 1920s).

Bob is fondly remembered in the town as a kindly and generous fellow who brought up a large family. It was said that, at the time of his diamond wedding, 100 of his descendants attended the celebrations. He died at the age of eighty in February 1954 and was interred in the new extension to the cemetery, his being the first burial there. His granddaughter was the celebrated actress Kay Kendall, whose name is now commemorated in the Lighthouse Museum in Hull Road, Withernsea.

The popular vogue for ultra-distance walking, which attracted many people of both sexes for monetary or purely altruistic reasons during the early part of the twentieth century, spawned many colourful characters such as the Iron Mask, Arizona Dan or the two Dutchmen Klaas and Piet.

One of these formidable men was the American George M Schilling from Pittsburg, Pennsylvania, who claimed to be the world's champion long-distance walker. He set off from New York in 1897 wearing only a suit made from newspapers and no money, and he had to exist by selling picture postcards of himself as part of a wager. After many adventures and suffering the vicissitudes of some bizarre foreign customs, he completed his marathon walk in 1905.

In March 1905, whilst in England on the final leg of his journey, he passed through Hull where he called in at the drapery establishment of Mr Christie on Anlaby Road to purchase some handkerchiefs. He was immediately attracted to the assistant Ellen May Matthews, who was twenty-three years of age. After a whirlwind romance they were married, much to the surprise of her family and friends, and departed for New York the next month.

Mr. GEORGE M. SCHILLING, THE FAMOUS AMERICAN ATHLETE, WHO IS WALKING ROUND THE WORLD FOR A WAGER, and who has walked 53,800 miles since August, 1897, left New York in a newspaper suit and penniless. He has walked through America, Australia, Asia, Africa, and has now completed his Tour in Europe, (except Ireland), and will arrive in New York in May, 1905.

Unfortunately George lost his wager by running out of time. He was severely held up by an attack of cholera in Egypt and imprisoned in Turkey. He did, however, receive monies representing the accumulated interest on the amount staked.

Trade and Industry

IT IS A RECOGNISED fact that the state of the economy at any given time has a direct bearing on the lifestyle and working conditions of people in all walks of life. Sometimes changes came about in a subtle inexplicable way, almost unnoticed by the average person, but at times changes occurred as a direct result of political moves by the government of the day. The First World War was one such politically influenced period.

The turn of the last century is generally agreed to be a major turning point in the history of this country, when the dominance won by the empire builders of the nineteenth century began almost imperceptibly to wane. In the years between 1900 and the end of the First World War, wages stopped rising — in some cases they fell slightly — but prices did rise. The upper classes prospered, partly due to the Empire and partly due to the expansion of mining and other industries. A new kind of social mobility gave the newly rich industrialists a status which would not under any circumstances have been acceptable to the highly class-conscious Victorians.

At the working-class level, the cottage industries such as weaving had been overtaken by the mills and factories. There were two levels of working man, the skilled and the unskilled. The unskilled were, unfortunately relegated to the ranks of underpaid cheap labour in all types of employment. Agriculture, which was one of the chief forms of employment in the East Riding, was not subjected to quite such a decisive structure, but it is true to say that many of the families just managed to live at what can only be described as subsistence level. In spite of this, many families lived contented lives, working hard both for employer and at producing their own food in cottage gardens. Many kept a pig which they fed on potato peelings and any other scraps which could not be used for the table. With frugal use of the meat and the by-products such as the dripping, the housewife could give some nourishment to her family in the cold winter months when the work on the land was particularly punishing for the men.

There were, of course, other rural pursuits such as the wheelwright and the farrier, to name but two. These skilled men were highly respected in the community and without exception they took a pride in their craftsmanship rarely found today.

Fishing was the prime occupation along the East Yorkshire coast. This usually involved the whole family. The father and his sons (as soon as they were old enough) went to sea, whilst the wives and daughters collected bait and baited hooks on the lines for the men to take out the next day. There were always nets to be mended, and the women were sometimes helped with this task by 'granddad', who was, often much to his disgust, declared by his sons as too old to go to sea. Where a family owned a boat, it was often shared by several brothers, implying a standard of affluence to those not familiar with life in a fishing community. The women of the family also knitted the 'ganseys' which most fishermen wore as a means of identification in case of disaster, most fishing regions having their own distinctive pattern. The life of the fisherfolk was hard and the rewards were few, but there was a great spirit in the communities. Many a woman who lost her man at sea could be sure that she and her children would not want for a roof over their heads, nor would they go hungry. In return she would help the women with the bait and nets.

The fishing fleet has provided employment for many in Hull for almost 150 years. In addition to the intrepid trawler men, the industry has employed large numbers of workers in maintaining the fleet, and the landing and distribution of the catch. There were also factories employed in box making, basket making, net making and other ancillary services. Between 1914 and 1918 the fishing fleet was badly depleted, but by 1939 it had been replenished and claimed to be the best in the world.

There was also work in rural areas through domestic service. To work at the 'big house' was a highly sought-after form of employment. Jobs were often found with the affluent families for a girl by a relative already in their employ. Similarly, a gardener or footman would try to find a place for his sons or nephews in some capacity; often, in the case of a footman, the lad would be found a job as a bootboy or some other menial position.

Opportunities for work in towns and urban areas were more varied, but for the working classes life was much harder. They did not have the means of producing their own food, but ironically, like their rural counterparts, many urban dwellers kept a pig, often in a tiny yard or cellar, and even in a spare room in a house. Gardens were practically unheard of, but when the Reckitt family conceived the idea for better housing, which culminated in the building of Garden Village in Hull, Sir James Reckitt's dream that each house should have a small garden to grow vegetables was fulfilled. This unique development was officially opened in 1908.

Towns were not as large or as densely populated as they are today, though many people were crowded into their close environs. Ports such as Hull offered employment on the docks for the men and low-paid factory work, often involving very long hours for the women. Some women, in order to raise their children, took in washing, for which they received very poor reward.

Having listed some of the major occupations of the East Riding, we have also included in this chapter some of the more unusual forms of employment such as the ferryman and the saddler, along with a few which will no doubt be familiar to many readers from their childhood days, a typical example being the ice-cream man with his special bicycle.

Facing page bottom: Foston on the Wolds. A typical picture of a Wolds village in the early part of the last century. On the left is the blacksmith's shoeing shed with the farrier and his son inside; the lady standing at the gate is the farrier's wife.

The horse was an integral part of life in the agricultural areas of Holderness. This is a typical farm cart in Easington, with ladders on the sides to increase the capacity of the load, from before the First World War.

This postcard was sent on the 3rd April 1937 to Messrs Geo Evans & Sons, rope and halter makers, 17¹/₂ Mytongate, Hull, from H Norris, saddle and harness maker of Keyingham. The message reads: 'Dear Sir, Will you please put on as early a buss as possible this morning 2 doz No 1 halters & ¹/₂ doz pony halters & 1 pair of breaking lines we want the halters for sale Mr Coates & they are wanting them badly. Yours H Norris.' An interesting point is that, in spite of the gentleman's trade, he is requesting delivery by bus. In the 1930s this was not an uncommon way of conveying parcels to the villages on the bus routes.

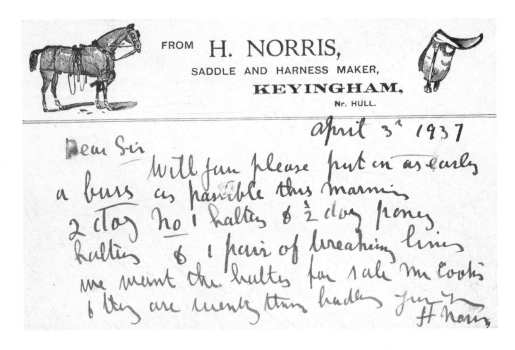

The making of saddles is a very ancient art, some of the earliest examples being attributed to the Mongolian nomads. When stirrups were added, this made the horse more effective as a means of transport, and also opened up the immense possibilities for the use of the horse in warfare. What is thought to be the oldest complete saddle is one used by Henry V and was carried at his funeral in 1422.

Collars are also an important item produced by the saddler who makes harness. When a heavy horse is pulling a plough or a load of hay, one admires the animal and thinks how well suited it is to the job, but a closer appraisal reveals that the collar takes the strain by distributing the load evenly across the shoulders where the muscular power originates, rather than on the neck. It was due to the introduction of the horse collar that the agrarian revolution during the Middle Ages was so successful, with far-ranging ramifications.

Harness has evolved in the same way over the centuries, like that for the drawing of a heavy vehicle such as a farm waggon. A set of harness included a headpiece, blinkers, nose band, rein and bit. Then came the collar, back band, crupper, breeching trace and belly band. Breaking lines were attached to the bridle by metal rings when training a young horse. These were two long ropes which could be used to steer the horse to left or right until it became accustomed to the harness.

Saddle making has always been a labour-intensive hand craft. Sadly, with the advent of the internal combustion engine, many saddlers turned to other forms of leather-work, but in agricultural areas such as the East Riding it was, and still is, a very necessary service.

Floyd Kirk and his beloved Blossom. Floyd was born at Burton Pidsea in 1909, but most of his youth was spent at Enholmes Hall, Patrington, where his father was head stockman. At the age of thirteen he moved to Danthorpe and a year later, on leaving school, went into service at Danthorpe Hall as a groom for the late Mr Henry Dixon.

The East Riding men who worked with horses either in agriculture or in the stables of the local gentry had one thing in common. They loved their horses with an intensity that is rarely to be found amongst hardworking men. Many are the stories of men who put the welfare and comfort of their horses before their own needs. Floyd was no exception, and often told how he would meet May, the girl who was to become his wife, and before they carried out their plans for the evening, they would both go to the stables to make sure that Blossom was happy and comfortable. Through-out his life he retained his deep love of horses, even though he no longer had daily contact with them.

Facing page: For nearly two centuries the fishermen of Filey have come from about a dozen families. These have constantly intermarried, thereby producing a tight-knit community. This is hardly surprising, as fisher families invariably lived in a few streets at the north end of the town, and it was essential that a fisherman should take a wife who knew what was expected of her and was already experienced in such skills as collecting bait and baiting the hooks. She should be able to repair nets, and knit the 'ganseys' or jerseys with their unique distinctive patterns which were worn by the men.

Gathering bait could be a long and arduous task in itself. A woman would often rise at five o'clock on a Monday morning and complete the family's washing before setting out, and often she would return after dark and still have to prepare the bait for the hooks. A fishwife's tasks in Filey also included collecting water from the ravine near St Oswald's Church to stock up the supply on the fishing cobles. Many also maintained the fishing gear and made sure that the oilskins were kept in serviceable order. And like any other housewife they cooked, cleaned and cared for their families, which were often quite numerous.

One wonders how they ever found time to knit the innumerable pairs of socks and several ganseys for their menfolk. In our photograph the lady is wearing a very neatly crocheted cape, so obviously the needlework was not solely produced for the men. As with the lifeboatmen, and indeed many rural occupations, it is obvious that a good wife was a treasure indeed, and many of these hardworking men were the first to admit that without their wives they would be lost.

Fishermen launching cobles at Filey.

SCALBY JACK=OF=ALL= TRADES.

A reader forwards an interesting advertisement relating to a late Scalby worthy, whose many sidedness is indicated in it. It has previously been published, but it will repay further perusal. It reads as follows:—" Enos Thompson, Scalby, near Scarborough. sexton, joiner, builder and undertaker, painter and grainer, whitewasher and paperhanger, plumber and glazier, whitesmith, locksmith, gasfitter and bellhanger, carver, gilder, and picture frame maker, watch and clock repairer, wheelwright, etc., begs to inform the clergy, gentry, and inhabitants of Scalby and neighbourhood that, having had considerable experience in the above branches of business, he will be glad to receive any orders entrusted to his care, and can with confidence assure them that such orders will receive his immediate and best attention, combined with punctuality, practical experience, and first class workmanship with moderate charges."

Above: Enos Thompson of Scalby would appear, from these details, to have been the answer to the needs of everybody. One cannot help but conjecture as to how he would fulfil his promise of 'immediate and best attention' and 'punctuality' if the response to his advertisement in the early part of the twentieth century had been commensurate with the services he offered.

Facing page top: In the herring season, Scottish fisher lasses followed the fishermen and shoals of fish down the East Coast as far as Lowestoft. All available space was utilised on the jetties and piers at Scarborough by these girls. It was regarded as one of the holiday pastimes to watch them 'gipping' or gutting the herrings. There is an atmosphere of intense industry in the picture, which probably explains the almost morbid interest in this odorous and somewhat unsavoury job by some of the visitors whom, one suspects, revelled in their leisure whilst watching others work. It was claimed that a fisher lass who was proficient at her job could gut up to fifty herrings a minute — or almost one every second.

Mrs Maria Horsley ran a general carrier service between Seamer and Scarborough three times a week for a number of years until shortly before her death in June 1914 aged eighty. Maria with her horse and cart was affectionately known by the locals as the 'Seamer Express'. This is a jocular reference to the fact that the short journey between the two places often took between three and four hours. Our photograph shows Mrs Horsley in Hanover Road, Scarborough, during the rail strike of 1911. Maria was then in her late seventies, and the horse looks equally aged.

Until the iron bridge was built between Goole and Howden in 1929, the only means of crossing the river was the ferry. This was operated by Robert Lightowler, the licensee of the Percy Arms, and his sons. (Opposite is a studio portrait of Mr and Mrs Lightowler.) The ferry saved many hours on a journey between Hull and Goole. Light loads of a few people were taken across in a rowing boat, whilst light vehicles were transported on a larger motor ferry. The ferry was summoned by the dubious means of calling from the opposite bank and waving one's handkerchief to attract attention. This must surely on occasion have led to frustration on the part of the would-be traveller if the ferryman was otherwise occupied.

Egg collecting was a very profitable occupation in the nineteenth century. It was carried out on the East Yorkshire coast by men from Flamborough and Bempton. It took place each year over a six-week period from mid-May to the end of June, when the guillemots laid their eggs.

The right of egg collecting belonged to the farmer whose land was on the clifftop, and he usually extended the right to the men who worked for him all year round. There were usually three or four gangs at work, taking an average of around 300 to 400 eggs a day. This meant that during the season it was possible to collect between 40,000 and 50,000 eggs. The price given for the eggs collected varied. Some were sold as cheaply as sixteen for a shilling (5p) and, at the other end of the scale, a well-marked rarer egg could fetch as much as 7s 6d (37½p). Most of the eggs were eaten, but some were used for wine clearing and as dressing for patent leather. If the weather was bad and delayed collecting, the eggs were still taken and fed to the pigs as this often made the birds lay again.

EGG CLIMBERS.

An iron bar was driven into the clifftop to anchor the rope. The climber also used a sling which encircled his waist and had two loops for his legs. This allowed the man to swing from ledge to ledge. One trick was to take a handful of grass to prevent the hands blistering on the ropes. The collector signalled to the men at the top by a series of jerks on his lifeline. The climber carried two bags on his shoulders and a stick with an iron hook. His somewhat incongruous headgear was a bowler hat, as shown in the group photograph, filled with padding to protect his head from falling stones. There were surprisingly few accidents, possibly because the men knew the climbs so well. At the end of the day the eggs were shared out equally.

Facing page: Ice-cream was part of most people's childhood. In the days of the trips to the seaside (often Sunday School treats and the like), even the poorest child would usually manage what was spoken of as 'a copper for an ice-cream'. Most ice-cream vendors in the early part of the century not only sold the delicious confection, but also made it, often under household conditions which, whilst perfectly clean, would have horrified today's health inspectors. They took a pride in the quality of their wares, and would endeavour to outdo each other with their claims to diplomas and medals awarded to their produce. Blythe Brothers were well known in Withernsea, having premises on Queen Street and also selling their ice-creams on the beach.

In the 1930s the 'Stop Me and Buy One' man was a familiar figure in all parts of the country. This method of selling ice-cream from a bicycle allowed for more sophisticated packaging. There were wrapped portions instead of scoops and pails of ice-cream, and new flavours were available which greatly appealed to the thirties generation who were looking for a 'modern' image.

Below: Dockers on strike in Hull in the summer of 1893. The famous Dock Strike of 1889 had paved the way for local disputes. Ben Tillett, John Burns, Tom Mann and Will Thorne had all been active as strike and union leaders, but it was Ben Tillett (1859–1943) who was the founder of the Dockers Union and its first secretary. A branch of the Dockers Union was formed in Hull in 1893 and the strike, which began in April, lasted six weeks.

A uniformed attendant at the famous Mortimer Museum, Hull. The curator was Thomas Sheppard, who was born in 1876 at South Ferriby. He began his working life as a railway clerk at the goods station in Kingston Street, Hull. His great interest was geology, and by 1903 was a member of several learned societies. In 1901 he was appointed curator of Hull's Municipal Museum in Albion Street.

The collection was the life work of J R and R Mortimer, corn merchants of Driffield. The collection consisted of around 60,000 archaeological exhibits and about 6,000 geological specimens which had been excavated by the brothers. The items were mainly Bronze Age and from East Yorkshire sites.

Sheppard desperately wanted the collection for Hull and worked very hard to secure it. The collection was originally housed in Driffield. When J R Mortimer died in 1911, he left a will saying that if the trustees could not keep the collection in Driffield, Hull should be given the opportunity to purchase it. In 1913, after long and protracted negotiations, a local man, Colonel G H Clarke, provided the £1,000 that Sheppard needed to secure the collection.

T S Kaye & Sons were a well-known tool-making business in Hull and Goole. Above are men at the Hull works sharpening bayonets in 1915 for soldiers in the trenches.

The coming of the railways to East Yorkshire was very important, bringing visitors to the seaside towns, and transporting produce from farm and factory. This group of railwaymen are standing by an engineers' van belonging to the North Eastern Railway around 1920.

Recreation and Leisure

THE PEOPLE OF THE East Riding were no exception to the prevailing conditions of the late Victorian and Edwardian periods, leisure being principally for the upper-middle classes and gentry.

Being a farming and fishing area, hard work was the lot of the average man and woman in the region. There was no way that the work could be halted — animals must be fed and watered even on Christmas Day — and the most ardent chapel-going farmer recognised that some work must be done on Sundays, and when harvesting began and timing was often crucial to beat possible bad weather, chapel had to be fitted in to accommodate the work. As with the farmers, the fishermen's lives were ruled by prevailing weather conditions and tides. Once the catch was landed, it had to be prepared and marketed, and the lines had to be baited for the next trip. In urban areas there was an occasional celebratory half-day holiday, and Sundays were not working days, but hours were long and money was scarce. In spite of these conditions, most people managed to find some form of enjoyment on the few occasions when there was an hour or two to spare.

Village green activities such as cricket matches, often organised by the local gentry, were popular in the country, there were also sports and athletics, sometimes arranged by the chapel, and held on the fields of obliging farmers. There were usually highly desirable prizes on offer at these events.

The Martinmas Feast on the 11th November was eagerly anticipated, as were the fêtes, garden parties and bazaars dear to the hearts of the Victorian and Edwardian ladies who appear to have been born organisers, and presumably filled some of their empty hours with committees and meetings aimed at the efficient running of these social events.

The railways ran trips to the seaside, particularly on Bank Holidays, but most weekends in summer the resorts were crowded. A week at the seaside was now a possibility for most middle-class families, and carnival weeks, which by the 1920s were held in most resorts, and from an earlier date the Scarborough Pageant, brought extra crowds to the town. A large number of people have devoted many hours and much hard work to the production of the pageant over the years, giving pleasure to thousands.

An event that was eagerly anticipated was the marriage of a member of the local gentry. At least a half-day's holiday would be declared and usually some kind of treat such as a tea in the village hall would be provided. Everyone turned out to watch the bride arrive and a festive air pervaded.

All classes spent some time of leisure in summer holding picnics. These ranged from a simple meal often outside, to very elaborate affairs with special stoves to make tea and large hampers of specially prepared food. Camping was also very popular, again with varying degrees of comfort.

In Holderness the feasts (now referred to as agricultural shows) were eagerly anticipated. 'Waggie' (chief horseman) would be in charge of a beautifully groomed pair of dressed horses and a cart. The 'lads' from each farm all helped in the hope of making their entry the best, and much-coveted prizes could be won. These shows had many attractions, the beer tent always being popular, and rich and poor mingled happily off the showground.

After the First World War the pattern changed to some degree, with more sophisticated forms of amusement now available. In towns, film shows were now being offered, and, in village hall, equally enjoyable magic lantern shows were very popular. The late 1920s saw the advent of the 'talkies', and even though it is claimed that this adversely affected the theatre and variety shows, the Pierrots still drew the crowds at the seaside.

Circuses were very popular, and a high spot across Holderness was the annual visit of Hull Fair to this bustling port, with its music, roundabouts and ubiquitous side shows. Trips were organised by the railways to give the rural population a chance to visit this unique gathering of bright lights, brash displays and universal fun.

There has also been a long-standing tradition of choirs and amateur theatricals throughout the region, giving sterling performances to a wide range of audiences.

By the 1920s some workers had graduated to a week's paid holiday from their place of employment, but this was by no means universal until the Holidays With Pay Act in 1938. Most took their holidays at home with the occasional day at the seaside, but in 1930 the Youth Hostel Association was started which made it possible for more young people to have a holiday. Also, by now middle-class families had a car and leisure time was an opportunity to 'go for a spin'.

During this period, gambling increased. Bets were made on horses, and from the late twenties, when the mechanical hare was introduced for greyhound racing, on the dogs. Football pools began in the 1930s, and many happy hours were spent assessing the odds and filling in the coupon, only to have one's hopes dashed each weekend after the Saturday evening ritual of listening to the football results on the wireless.

Some of the leisure pursuits mentioned are still available today, but in this age of technology, sadly, they do not in the main afford the enjoyment they gave to our parents and grandparents.

Young music-makers from Easington, including a pianist, five violinists and three vocalists. Note the knee-high laced boots worn by the young lady next to the pianist.

Hedon School Feast was the highlight of the year for most children of the town in the early part of the last century. It was a matter of pride with mothers that their child should be 'well turned out' for the parade. It is easy to imagine the consternation of fathers and older brothers as the house became littered with garments in all stages of finish, and bits and pieces to decorate hats. In some families the materials would be new, but in the poorer houses, dresses of larger size would be unpicked and recut. If a member of the family was in domestic service, this may possibly be a good quality cast-off garment from her employers. The adults, too, liked to show off their best on Feast Sunday.

The children took produce to the church, later to be distributed to the poor, and then the parade with its banners would begin. After a short service, the parade was led from the church by the band to the grounds of Ivy House, where there would ensue an afternoon of fun and games.

On Monday there was another parade, this time with gaily decorated carts. This proceeded to the board School where a feast had been prepared for the children. It then headed for the cricket ground where there were stalls and side shows, most having saved their pennies for this treat. There were sports, with all the usual fun races such as the sack and egg-and-spoon. The festivities continued well into the evening, and it is easy to imagine over-excited, tired children being carried home on dad's shoulders after a day to be remembered, until it came around next year.

Our picture shows some of those taking part in 1910, but the event was still being organised in the early 1930s.

Above: When the railways between Hull and the coastal resorts were opened, one of the popular leisure pursuits was a cheap day trip to the seaside. This view of the promenade at Hornsea supports this statement: people are enjoying the sea air, and some are walking along the 'prom', often hailing friends who have had the same idea themselves. There was plenty of diversion for those who wished to be amused, including the usual beach amenities, and there were the Pierrots (possibly Harry Russell's) and numerous joys on offer at the Floral Hall. For those so minded, a happy hour could be passed 'looking round the shops' or just having 'a bit of peace and quiet' in the park.

Donkey rides have always been part of the enjoyment of a seaside holiday. Many young visitors saved titbits from their meals for these patient creatures, and having obtained permission from the owners, took great pleasure in feeding their forbearant friends. In many seaside towns the donkeys were owned by members of the same family for decades, and became friendly with the children who came year after year for rides and to pet the donkeys. This young rider on Filey beach, ably supported by mum, has obviously begun riding at an early age, possibly in anticipation of future pleasures.

Facing page bottom: This picture of Scarborough was obviously taken before the 8th January 1905 because, as a result of a storm during the previous night, the pier had been destroyed. In 1887-8 the land behind the pier had been landscaped and made into pleasing gardens complete with bandstand. This was known as Clarence Gardens. The people here are obviously enjoying a band performance, but there were also Pierrot shows. Will Catlin stored his costumes in a kiosk in the garden, which was completely destroyed — along with Will's costumes — in the bombardment of 1914.

The South Cliff Tramway at Scarborough claimed to be the first cliff railway in England. Opened in 1875, it linked the Esplanade to the Spa. Gradually it proved a great amenity to holidaymakers who, perhaps not in the first flush of their youth, spent much of their time around the Spa area either taking in the air or listening to the band. It was also very popular with young visitors, if they could persuade parents that it was essential to find pennies to take the family to the top from the beach and so enjoy the thrill of viewing the scene from above as the car ascended. A similar amenity was eventually provided at the North Bay opposite the famous Corner Café in 1929.

Camping became a craze during the early part of the twentieth century for young men. This relaxed group have pitched their bell tent at Easington, but are characteristic of campers in all parts of Britain. For a few days they lived in a primitive manner, carrying out their ablutions with the help of water in buckets — shaving under such conditions, especially with the old cut-throat razors, must have proved perilously uncomfortable. They cooked rudimentary meals over a primus-type stove and, we were told, consumed large quantities of bread and cheese 'cos it was easy'. They filled their time with such pursuits as hiking, or if their chosen site was near the sea, swimming, beachcombing and a little fishing. The customary evening pastime was to retire to the local hostelry.

Dr Coates of Patrington, who is documented on page 5 of our personalities chapter, had a beach hut at Kilnsea. This was referred to by the good doctor as 'our flat'. It was on the sandy shore in the area between Kilnsea and Spurn, and sited on the grass which grew along the edge of the peninsular. Dr Coates has gone on record as declaring himself the cook, and producing a creditable menu whilst the rest of the party was responsible for the washing up on the beach. This involved scrubbing the plates and pans with clean, dry sand, and, after passing his eagle-eyed scrutiny, they were dried on the stove. This photograph was taken in 1906, and the family used the 'flat' throughout the summer months, with the doctor visiting at the weekends. It was, apparently, a common sight to see the beds laid out on the sand to air.

Facing page bottom: The charabanc — from the French *char à bancs* meaning carriage with benches — became very popular in the 1920s for social outings. This was a large, long motor vehicle with transverse seats and an open top, popularly known as a 'sharra'. Our picture shows happy holidaymakers with a Cottingham-based vehicle, well known in the area. The passengers were usually an arranged party, perhaps from a church or chapel, or sometimes the vehicle was hired out for a works outing, the cost of which would be defrayed by the organisers or the passengers themselves. Private parties would also hire a charabanc, the shared cost of the trip rendering such outings not only possible but very reasonable, thus ensuring an enjoyable day out.

Bridlington's Floral Pavilion was built in 1904 and was an extremely popular venue for both residents and visitors. This beautiful glass and metal construction, which true to its name was always tastefully decorated with hanging baskets filled with flowers and plants providing a riot of colour, could seat around 2,000 people. Plants were also strategically placed to add to the conservatory atmosphere. It was noted for its musical concerts, the entertainment being always of the highest standard — indeed, orchestras and musicians were always eager to perform at the Pavilion.

After the strictures of the late Victorian era, Edward VII was very popular with his subjects. He changed the whole concept and appeal of the monarchy, and is said to have been arguably England's most popular king for many centuries.

He was born in 1841 but did not accede to the throne until 1901. His appeal appears to stem from the fact that, whilst always ready to meet his responsibilities politically and otherwise, he knew how to enjoy life. He has been described as a tolerant and affable man, and is said to have fitted the image of the typical Englishman of the period. Some of his more recondite exploits included attending cockfighting and ratting contests. He was a keen supporter of the turf and enjoyed his racing, his most famous victory was probably the 1909 Derby when his horse Minoru came home first. His other most noteworthy peccadillo was an eye for the ladies.

He was always enthusiastic about house parties, and seems to have been quite partial to Yorkshire. Many are familiar with the Tranby Croft Scandal in which Edward the Prince of Wales was involved. During a game of cards, one of the players, Lt Col Sir William Gordon Cumming, was accused of cheating by two younger players. Cumming denied this and took out a court action, which he subsequently lost. The prince had to be called as a witness and was forced to admit to have been playing an illegal card game. Tranby Croft was the home of the well-known Hull shipowners, the Wilson family.

But it is not so well known that the king favoured Londesborough Hall, where he is shown enjoying an informal ride. Whilst staying in the area the local people welcomed his public appearances, and his arrivals and departures were an excuse for social gatherings. As he would wave and beam affably at such a gathering, inevitably the cry would go up 'Good Old Teddie'.

All royal occasions have been a time of enjoyment or leisure, often being celebrated by a half holiday, but the people in the areas closely connected with royalty speak of them with respect but in a manner that might apply to a member of one's family.

A society wedding. The bride is Miss Elizabeth Gertrude Coates, daughter of Dr and Mrs W H Coates. The bridegroom is Gerald Edward Sykes, son of Mr and Mrs W Sykes of Cottingham. The wedding took place on the 21st July 1911 at Patrington Church, which was beautifully decorated with palms and ferns. Over 200 guests were invited to lunch at Bleak House. They were entertained to a lunch provided by Powolneys of Hull, and the music was played by Herr Blome's Bijou Orchestra. The whole of Patrington village celebrated the event. There were teas for everyone and gifts for the children. Free film shows were provided at the temperance hall and the assembly rooms. It was often the case that the local gentry provided for the village to mark such occasions as weddings in the family.

The bride's dress was of ivory mousseline with silver and lace trimmings. She carried a bouquet of orange blossom, white heather and white roses. Her bridesmaids, Miss Norah Vickerman of Sunk Island and Miss Mabel Mumby of Hull, wore gowns of pale mauve satin, with straw hats lined with mauve and trimmed with white lace and bunches of sweet peas, and both carried bouquets of sweet peas. They also wore brooches of gold and pearls which were a present from the Bridegroom. The little trainbearer is Miss Marjory Spikins. The bride's mother wore wedgewood blue and the bridegroom's mother favoured fawn satin. The good doctor is seen at the right of the group.

Fox hunting was a very popular pastime in the rural East Riding, which proved ideal with the flat landscape and plenty of areas of cover. The Holderness Hunt are pictured gathering at Beverley around 1908.

A proud owner shows off his horse decorated to celebrate the exploits of the Hull aviatrix, Amy Johnson. The parades and other celebrations of Amy's achievements added to the leisure enjoyment of many local people during the 1930s.

Feast day was the highlight of the village year in many places. It was eagerly anticipated by all age groups. This beautifully turned-out pair of working horses were to be seen at the Hutton Cranswick Feast in 1911.

The hired lads on a farm were responsible for a pair of horses, and in many cases felt a personal pride in their charges. At feast time there was a great rivalry to exhibit the winning pair. The lads would sometimes feed their horses with items such as raw eggs for several days before the feast to give the coat a glossy appearance. There was much energy spent on brushing and combing, and feet were washed and hooves polished on the evening before the great day. Work on the day itself began very early. Tails and manes were plaited with brightly coloured braids, garlands were made to bedeck them, and, of course, the beautiful brasses which had been burnished to perfection completed the picture. A surprising fact is that these were often bought by the lads, and not as might be expected by the masters.

The carts also received much attention and there were coveted prizes to be won. After the judging, the prizes were usually presented by a member of the local gentry, and the master (owner of the horses) would reward the lucky winners. It was customary for the man's family or relatives if he was unmarried to join him on the cart at this stage.

On feast day, everyone wore their best clothes and joined in the many entertaining activities on offer.

A very important meeting took place in Scarborough on the 22nd February 1911. The business to be discussed was the proposed production of a historical pageant. There was much influential support for the idea, and there was unanimous agreement that Castle Hill would be the ideal site for the performance.

It was decided that the pageant, spanning 800 years of local history, should be staged in July 1912. It was to be a five-day event which would involve 1,800 local people in varying capacities. The backstage jobs would number 500, whilst the rest had parts of varying importance in the actual performance. The pageant master was Mr Gilbert Hudson, who had produced other such events at Thirsk and Pickering, although not on such a large scale as this mammoth undertaking.

After a heavy shower of rain on the Monday morning of the first day, the sun shone brilliantly and the week commenced in grand style. The book of the pageant had fourteen episodes, which predictably began with a prologue and closed with an epilogue. It began in prehistoric times with a family quarrel, continued through Roman times (see facing page top) and the Druids, then moved on to the sacking of Scarborough by the Vikings, then naturally followed the history of the castle. The Cistercians and Franciscans were portrayed, and as the pageant reached episode six there was a magnificent spectacle of Edward I holding court. Then followed the defence of Scarborough by Piers Gaveston against the barons. The visit of Richard III in 1484 was enacted with the granting of the charter and commissions. In 1554 the castle was taken by Thomas Stafford, and the surrender of the castle to the Parliamentarian forces was depicted, culminating with the discovery of the spa waters by Mistress Farrow. The last episode was much more serene, telling of George Fox who was the last notable prisoner to be kept in the castle; he was the founder of the Society of Friends or Quakers, and served a term of one year and three months. The epilogue was spectacular. The fully assembled company sang the *Song of Scarborough*, and the spectators joined in the singing of the hymn *O God Our Help* and the national anthem. This was followed by a grand march-past of the company.

Throughout the week the route to the castle was lined with people waiting to catch sight of the performers, and from 2 pm to 7 pm Castle Road was thronged with hopeful onlookers. The price of a seat in the stands was 2s 6d (12½p) which in 1912 was quite expensive, so those who could not afford the admission charges contented themselves with glimpses of some of the cast, as our photograph below shows, and the sound of the music and fanfares which could be heard over a wide area.

Fairs were held in many towns and villages at Martinmas in November, and at other festivals such as Harvest and the May celebrations.

The gallopers have always been a popular ride. Complete with organ churning out rousing marches and bright waltzes, and animated carved figures to add to the enjoyment, the brightly coloured horses — each with a name — careered round on their barley-sugar twisted poles of polished chrome or brass. Many who could not afford a ride took pleasure in the music and the panoply of racing colours, and the sound of the carefree fairgoers.

Hull Fair, of course, has always been the event of the year for multitudes of East Yorkshire folk, but these small rural events with their limited attractions nevertheless gave many a chance they would not have been able to afford in other circumstances to enjoy 'All the Fun of the Fair'.

The year is 1932, and Withernsea's Carnival Parade, the crowning event of Carnival Week, is making its way along Pier Road towards Queen Street on its tour of the town, headed by Withernsea Brass Band.

The three small girls at the front were daintily dressed, and many an observer must have remarked how pretty they looked. No one at this date could have realised that the young lady in the middle, Justine McCarthy, with her sister Kim on one side and her cousin Jill Dootson on the other, was to become world famous. She was, of course, none other than Kay Kendall, who starred in many films but sadly died of leukaemia in 1959 aged thirty-three. Her sister Kim, had a successful stage career, but eventually married and went to live in America.

Withernsea Carnival has always been popular with both visitors and residents, traditionally taking place during the first week in August. The parade is preceded by a week of events including the crowning of the carnival queen and princess, and a host of fun activities for both young and old alike. The first carnival was staged in the mid-1920s and the event still takes place in the town today.

In the 1930s it is said that, during Carnival Week, boarding houses and hotels were bursting at the seams, and if the weather was good it was not unknown for some of the more hardy who either could not find or could not afford accommodation to sleep on the beach. This was typical of many resorts in all parts of Britain. There would be several bands to escort the horse-drawn floats. Sometimes the parade would have a theme, but some preferred to leave the choice to the participants. Fancy dress was always well represented, and if one won a prize that was the highlight of the week, something to be proudly shown off at school when the holidays were over.

When the circus came to town it brought numerous joys. The elephants always walked through the town after being released from their conveyances. This was doubly advantageous for the showmen: it solved the knotty problem of moving these gigantic plodding pachyderms through the streets, and was also an excellent advertisement for the forthcoming show. These elephants are crossing the old Monument Bridge in Hull during the first decade of the twentieth century. The crowd are obviously enjoying the spectacle, some being very precariously perched on nearby buildings. Usually they were accompanied by clowns and jugglers and other attractions to whet the appetite of the onlookers in the hope of attracting large numbers into the Big Top for the performances.

Facing page: There has been a castle on this hill in Scarborough since the Iron Age. The Romans in their turn also realised its potential as an unassailable site, but it was Henry II who really developed the castle as a royal stronghold. It was he who gave the community a charter, and thus it flourished as a fishing and trading port. He also strengthened the curtain wall of the derelict castle and built the square stone keep, the ruins of which still dominate the town. King John, Edward I and Richard III all had associations with the castle. Our picture, taken in 1911, shows a band descending the steps at the south side of the castle to Foreshore Road. Some spectators have ventured on to the steps at the side to enjoy the parade, getting an unimpaired view.

The Progressive Angling Association, whose members are pictured here with a splendid trophy, were participants in what has always been the most popular sport in Britain. This group of working men, like many of their contemporaries, engaged in the art of coarse fishing in river, canal, lake and pond. Angling had the added benefit of requiring little in the way of equipment, and the many waterways of East Yorkshire were readily accessible. It could be a solitary or group pursuit, with the added bonus of competitions and prizes, and fishermen could spend as much or as little time as they wished sitting on the riverbank. Our picture was taken by W Moody of Drypool, Hull.

In Times of Trouble

BRITAIN HAS ALWAYS BEEN famed for its 'stiff upper lip' when faced with adverse circumstances. There have been many derogatory remarks and mirthful references to this so-called national trait, but basically the nation has always commanded the respect of the world for stoicism in the face of misfortune.

In Yorkshire this stoicism shows itself to a degree beyond normal expectations. The county has, over the years, had its share of natural disasters such as floods and all forms of freak weather. It has, like all areas of Britain, suffered the effects of war and its accompanying sorrows. The coastline has a history of tragic shipwrecks, and there have also been notable fires. In the midst of all these major upheavals have been the lesser events which were perhaps more personal but none the less traumatic.

One becomes aware that when faced with a disaster of some proportion, such as the severe flooding which has occurred in many areas of Holderness, the people involved very quickly became an integral part of the community. People who consider themselves 'quite ordinary' respond to adversity with extreme courage and resourcefulness. Not only does such an event affect those personally involved, but those who are physically untouched, on hearing of a catastrophe, often feel a sense of vulnerability which motivates them to offer aid and comfort to the victims.

In Yorkshire there exists a kind of pride which produced an attitude of 'keeping to oneself' which can be interpreted as a form of fierce independence. In the event of a need for resources or aid for members in the immediate community, an attitude of share and share alike is adopted. Reserves are dropped (even if resumed when the emergency has receded), and warmth and kindness abound, along with practical help towards rehabilitation.

On a lesser scale there has always been a tradition of neighbour helping neighbour. Many are the stories of a farmer who falls ill and his neighbours tend his land and animals until he is well and active again. If there was a death in the family, even though they were all possibly living just above subsistence level, friends and neighbours would give what they could in the way of food for the funeral meal 'to put the deceased away proper'. Among the fishing community, if a woman lost her husband at sea, she and the 'bairns' were helped along with fish from the catches, and even if the diet was somewhat restricted at least they were not left to starve.

It is with this kindliness, which is often well hidden under a gruff Yorkshire exterior, and a tenacious attitude to survival that the people of the East Riding have overcome the misfortunes which, through circumstances beyond their control, have been their lot over the years.

Selby Abbey was originally a Bene-
dictine monastery. It was founded by a
monk called Benedict who came
from Auxerre in France in the reign of
William the Conqueror. It is said that
William's third son Henry, who was
later to become Henry I, was born at
Selby. By a strange coincidence the
abbey was founded in 1069, in 1690
the main tower fell down and
destroyed the transept, and as our
photographs show, it suffered severe
damage by fire in 1906.

The nave of Selby Abbey after the 1906 conflagration.

Howden Church dates back to the thirteenth century and is dedicated to Canon John, a local saint. There is a very tall tower which is said to have been built in such a manner to shelter people from floods. Fortunately this tower was not damaged in a fire which was started by an arsonist. The picture shows some of the damage caused on the 9th October 1929. The Saltmarsh Chapel escaped the conflagration, as did the family vault below. The nearby bishop's palace, which was built for the bishop of Durham, testifies to its importance as a collegiate church.

This scene of devastation shows the ruined municipal buildings in Withernsea which were destroyed by fire in 1913. In the picture is Mr Goulding whose nearby business narrowly escaped the conflagration. Mr Martin Cheverton Brown, a prominent financier, who lived in Withernsea and was chairman of the council on four occasions, the last being the year previous to the fire, eventually sold his large house in Queen Street to the council. It is still used as the town's municipal building.

The date was Friday the 20th May 1910. This was the day set for the funeral of King Edward VII, but for the people of Driffield and the surrounding villages, it has more dramatic associations.

At a little after 4 am a storm broke of such severity that the whole area was devastated. There was a flash after flash of vivid lightning, coupled with a continuous roar of thunder which caused the houses to vibrate. At 4.20 am, hailstones of prodigious size rained down. It was claimed that many were as large as pigeon eggs, and terrified cows and horses in the fields, causing them to charge around in pain. There was torrential rain, and soon the streets of the town had become rivers and water raced through the houses to collect in the slight valley in the centre of the town.

A theory has been proposed that the storm was connected with the recent passage of Halley's Comet between the earth and the sun. The villages of Lutton, Helperthorpe, Weaverthorpe, Butterwick, Cowlam and Langtoft were also badly affected.

It was estimated at the time of the flood that in excess of 150 homes were ruined, some families losing all their possessions. A child, Dora Whitehead, daughter of Thomas Whitehead of Providence Row, Driffield, was drowned but mercifully the infant was the only fatality.

The flat expanses at Kilnsea have always been the victim of flooding, especially when heavy storms pound this narrow strip of land. This was one of the reasons why it was considered better for the lifeboatmen who originally lived at Kilnsea to move to Spurn.

On Monday the 6th March 1906, the Yorkshire coast was swamped by one of the most devastating tides within living memory. Kilnsea, Spurn and Easington suffered dreadfully, and the effects were so disastrous it was feared that it would take several years for the land to recover sufficiently to be used for agricultural purposes. The floods could not have occurred at a worse time for the farmer, as the crops were just beginning to germinate and were completely destroyed, and the land was impregnated with the salt water, rendering it unsuitable for immediate resowing. It is said that the gulls were the only creatures to benefit when the waters subsided, leaving behind rich pickings in the form of dead worms. Many acres of land were submerged — the water in some parts was reported to be between five and eight feet (1.5-2.5m) deep — and people were made homeless.

Whilst this area was the worst hit, the storm caused havoc right down the coast. Marine Drive at Scarborough was submerged and the North Pavilion damaged, a ship was wrecked off Bridlington, at Hornsea the promenade suffered, Withernsea escaped serious damage but Grimston and Turnstall suffered. The tail end of the storm caused minor flooding in Cleethorpes, and Barton suffered from the high tide in the Humber. Even as far inland as Selby the Ouse overflowed, causing some flooding in the town.

Mr Stanley Wilson, MP for Holderness, called the attention of the President of the Board of Trade to the plight of the people of Kilnsea and surrounding areas, and the urgency of providing aid and sea defences.

Spurn or 'Spon', as it was once referred to locally, has had a lifeboat since 1810. The first boat was housed in a disused barracks, and when there was an alarm the men had to come from Kilnsea and Easington as quickly as possible. Inevitably this caused delays, and in 1819 Trinity House built a row of cottages with money raised by public subscription so that the men who manned the boat could now live on the peninsular. Unfortunately these cottages were badly placed and were exposed to the full blast of the elements. A further row of houses was built in 1857-8, but even in these, with a strong westerly wind blowing, the spray came over the rooftops and the windows had to be shuttered. The lifeboatmen were fishermen and helped to keep their families by beachcoming for salvage blown ashore from ships. Their pay for lifeboat duties was brought to them by the coxswain once a month.

In 1895, Spurn Lighthouse was built and the keepers fared a little better than those on the rock lighthouse. There was the Lifeboat Inn where survivors of the many wrecks were cared for as they were brought ashore, and sadly on occasion served as a mortuary.

The Spurn lifeboatmen have always had a reputation for extreme bravery, and on many winter nights, with a howling northerly gale blowing, these men would be called from the comfort of their beds. A man's wife would help him into his oilskins and lifejacket. As the crew carried the boat out and began to row, there must have been many anxious hearts as the women kept a solemn vigil until the dawn revealed how their men had fared, and if a rescue had been affected. Lifeboatmen all along the East Yorkshire coast have over the years won many awards for bravery beyond the course of duty, but one feels that perhaps the women were equally commendable. It was they who suffered the torments of not knowing if their men would come home to them, and in some cases the ultimate heartbreak of losing a husband, son, father or brother, since many lifeboat crews were composed of more than one member of a family. Our photographs shows a typical Spurn crew in oilskins and lifejackets.

Strong winds and rough seas were a menace to seaside piers all around the coast of the British Isles. It has been claimed that these Victorian 'fun amenities' were directly responsible for the loss of many lives, as ships found it impossible in the high winds to avoid these constructions.

None of the piers originally erected on the Yorkshire coast survived the 'big blows' of the 1880s unscathed and, by the early part of the twentieth century, very little remained to show they had ever existed. After a ship collision in 1883, which caused extensive damage, Scarborough Pier was washed away overnight in 1905. Both Hornsea and Withernsea piers were seriously shortened by storm damage in 1880. After continuous battering by heavy seas, Hornsea was derelict by 1897 and demolished by 1910.

Like Hornsea, Withernsea lost 200 feet (60m) when on the night of the 22nd and 23rd October 1880 the coal barge *Saffron* was blown off course, and passed through the pier and ended up on the shore. On that fateful night, fifty ships were in difficulties between Spurn and Bridlington as a result of the storm, and nine were wrecked. Many lives were lost and much of the coastal area was flooded. This gravestone in St Nicholas's churchyard, Withernsea, commemorates George Kettle aged forty-one, George Fitch aged twenty-one, William Gant aged eighteen, and James John Lumb aged thirty-three (who was interred at nearby Holmpton), natives of Colchester who were drowned in the storm of the 23rd October 1880. Withernsea Pier suffered further storm damage in 1882, and by 1893 there was only 50 feet (15m) remaining of the original 1,200 feet (365m). This was ignominiously removed, leaving only the splendid pier towers and gates.

On the 21st October 1904 (Trafalgar Day) the Russian Outrage, or as it is officially named the Dogger Bank Incident, took place. The Russian naval fleet fired on a group of Hull trawlers under the misconception that they were Japanese naval ships, Russia being at war with Japan at that time. Six trawlers were hit, causing injury to several men. The captain of the *Crane*, George Henry Smith, was killed, leaving a widow and eight children, and ship's hand William Leggett, a twenty-eight year old bachelor, was also killed.

The incident caused national consternation, but the people of Hull were incensed. This is reflected (below) by the vast crowds lining Spring Bank on the 27th October 1904 as the coffins made their stately way through the streets accompanied by three bands who simultaneously played the solemn *Dead March*. The mayor can be seen at the head of the procession wearing his chain of office, followed by the flower-bedecked coffins. An eyewitness described the highly charged, emotional occasion as heartbreaking, with hardly a dry eye amongst the crowds.

The two graves (see opposite) have identical headstones recording the tragic details of the men's deaths, one erected by Captain Smith's wife and the other by William Leggett's mother. Both have a depiction of a trawler, and are surmounted by an ornate carving of an anchor.

The people of Hull generously subscribed for the erection of the famous statue of a fisherman which rests on the Boulevard as their tribute to the men. There are numerous pictures of the statue and also such souvenirs as crested china models.

In July 1921 the R38 arrived at Howden Airship Station for trials. It had been designed during the First World War as an answer to the German Zeppelins, but was finished too late and subsequently sold to the US Navy, who re-designated it the ZR2. Its first test flight at Cardington in Bedfordshire where it was built had revealed a number of faults, and it was hoped that these could be eradicated. Unfortunately, possibly due to the insistences of the Americans who were becoming homesick, the test programme was cut from 150 to 50 hours. Final modifications were to be made at Howden.

On a summer afternoon in August, the airship was sighted to the north-west of the city of Hull. People paused on their way home from work, and others emerged from shops and houses, to watch the airship as it headed towards the River Humber. Many described it as a beautiful sight. Suddenly, to the horror of everyone watching, the ship appeared to buckle and there was a loud explosion. Flames began licking the ship as thirty tons of petrol exploded, showering the river with burning fuel. As the R38 hit the murky water, the town was rocked by a further explosion. This was at exactly 5.38 pm. The unburnt tail section drifted towards Victoria Pier. On the shore there were still high hopes of rescue, but the boats were hampered by burning fuel. Only the captain Flight Lieutenant Wann was brought out alive from the bow section, and four men survived in the tail. Of the forty-nine on board, only five had survived. On shore, windows were shattered, and cycles and other stationary objects were hurled into the road. There were emotional scenes as charred bodies were brought to the pier. It is thought that those not killed by the explosion were drowned.

There has never been a satisfactory answer to the reasons for the tragedy. The skipper is recorded as saying that, whilst the ship was over the town, nothing was wrong and the disaster suddenly occurred without warning. A court of enquiry suggested 'insufficient attention to aerodynamic forces', but this was vague and did not really explain anything. There were murmurings about the cutting of the test programme, but no real answer had been forthcoming. There is a memorial to the victims in Hull Western Cemetery.

As is the habit of small (and so many not so small) boys, bits of the airship were collected as souvenirs. Many of these were made into attractive ornaments and souvenirs including ashtrays, candlesticks and small cast models of the R38. Much of the dull silver fabric survived and was made into purses and the like.

A slightly unusual disaster is recorded on a gravestone in Easington church-yard. The stone was erected to the memory of John Green Loftus, aged thirty-three of Hull. John was the mate of the brig *Express*, and fell from the vessel as she was entering the River Humber at the end of a voyage from St Petersburg in Russia. The accident occurred on the 18th May 1836, and his body was washed ashore at Kilnsea on the 4th June and was interred at Easington. Although comparatively young, he left a widow and four children who mourned him with the following verse:

'And is he gone who we so dearly loved
Whose tender kindness we so often prove.
Yes he is gone, his happy spirit fled,
And now he's numbered with the silent dead.'

Church and Chapel

THE RELATIONSHIP OF THE Church with the people around the end of the nineteenth century was a complex one. The different denominations pursued their aims according to their individual dogmas, thereby influencing the strata of society to which they ministered. In some cases the Church inspired a kind of self-discipline embodying hard work and temperance which, if carried out to the letter, could lead to a modicum of success in life. It has been suggested that perhaps the Church or Chapel provided a form of consolation by offering an alternative to a lifestyle which was often very hard.

In the early years of the reign of Edward VII, church attendance was very much a minority habit, but most children attended Sunday school, and women were more inclined to attend a service than men. The Anglican Church appealed to a wide range of social classes, but in many small communities the chapel held sway. In rural areas such as the East Riding, whilst many did truly believe, there were a number who attended church or chapel because the farmer or mistress for whom they worked insisted on it.

Both in rural and urban communities, regular attenders from the poorer classes were given such items as clothing and blankets, and on occasion, coal in winter. Treats were provided for the children in the form of outings in summer, and gifts and parties in winter. These were administered by middle-class and upper-class parishioners who regarded it as their Christian duty.

The Nonconformists divided roughly into Congregationalists and Wesleyans who were predominantly 'well-to-do' lower-middle-class Baptists and working-class Primitive Methodists.

The provision of entertainments and charity could not, and did not, hold a congregation, and the majority of the working classes used the churches and chapels for weddings, christenings and funerals. The Nonconformists appear to have made more of an effort to attract their parishioners than the Anglican or Catholic churches, the Church of Rome being assured of attendance and increasing numbers due to the very nature of their beliefs.

Chapels were built in profusion at this period and, whilst many were of solid or sober appearance, an almost vulgar style of architecture began to be used. There were often colourful signs and decoration, giving the impression that they were trying to compete with the music halls. Participation in the running of the chapel was encouraged, giving scope to those of the middle classes who liked to be seen as holding office. More popular pursuits were fostered such as football and dancing, and in the period prior to the First World War they began to sponsor the Scout movement and Boys' Brigade, reasonably considering that if they commanded the respect of the young members of a family, the adults would follow.

In the first decade of the twentieth century, there was a movement towards religious activity in the form of travelling evangelists on the gospel waggons, whose aim was to bring 'the word of the Lord' to the people. Some ministers frowned on these extemporaneous meetings, as a good evangelist fired with Biblical rhetoric could invoke what we now call mass hysteria. Nevertheless they won many true converts for the Church including drunkards, gamblers and perpetrators of other vices. Some of these renegades themselves became accomplished preachers, often quoting their own wretched lives that were once corrupt in the rampant miasma of transgression. It has been said that the oratory skills of some of these fervent tub-thumpers influenced the early founders of the Labour Movement, and the flamboyant style of presentation and eloquence of phrase used by these preachers was applied to the hustings in the early elections in which they contended.

It is generally accepted that the decline of religion in all faiths — Anglican, Catholic and Nonconformist — was brought about by a diversity of new influences in the 1920s and 1930s which arose from the steady growth of the mass media.

The Primitive Methodist Chapel at Beverley. Note the Spotted Cow public house next door.

Albert Shakesby, who was born in Hull around 1873, has been recognised as one of the most effective Evangelists of the early part of the twentieth century, being particularly successful in the East Riding.

His father was a drunkard, and his mother worked as a washer woman in an attempt to provide food for her children. Albert became an errand boy for a man who worked at the Cow Cake Mills in Hull. One of his jobs was to fetch hot suppers for the men who worked on the night shift, and he was often so hungry that he stole parts of the meals. He had very little schooling, and up to the time of his conversion was illiterate. When he was seven years of age his mother moved the family to Sunderland, where Albert, having no settled home, described himself as 'like a street Arab'. He sold boot laces, swept street crossings and blacked boots. He also drifted into petty crime, and admitted that he had 'seen inside of a prison more than once'.

On the fateful evening of the 9th January 1909, Albert was in a euphoric mood, having just won a prize in a music hall, and went to the Great Thornton Street Primitive Methodist Chapel with the intention of disrupting the meeting. The service was being conducted by Mr and Mrs Albert Harrison. When spoken to by Mrs Harrison, he replied rudely and told her he had a prizefight on the Wednesday. She told him he would not figure in this battle, and he gripped her hand with the intention of injuring her, but strangely his arm became powerless. These words haunted him, rendering him incapable of eating or sleeping. On the night of the prizefight he dressed for the contest, but his arms were powerless and hung by his sides. He turned his back on the jeering crowd of spectators and went back to the chapel, and after kneeling at the communion rail, his conversion was completed. He saved his first soul that very evening, his own wife.

From then on he renounced all his previous doubtful activities, and preached in many East Yorkshire chapels including Scarborough, Filey, Bridlington, and Patrington. His sermons drew large congregations, largely to listen to his inspired rhetoric, and he made many converts.

Grice Jackson was born at Owthorne in 1822. He is said to have started work at the age of five, tending cattle and pigs owned by his parents at Cherry Cobb Sands. As agricultural labourer was the only employment available in the area, he became a farmer's boy, working long hours from 5 am to 8 pm for very little remuneration. At the age of eighteen he married. His wife's parents were farmers at Hatfield near Sigglesthorne, and he lived at their farm, finding for the first time a settled home. Marriages in those days were not performed after noon, and having decided that they would marry at Swine, he set out very early on foot to walk the five miles (8km). Even so, he only just managed to place the ring on his bride's finger by noon.

His life at Hatfield was very happy, but when he heard of the building of a local railway, he decided that was for him, and he moved with his wife and household effects to Withernsea on a donkey and cart. As there were few roads, the way lay across the farmers' fields and tolls had to be paid. Having rested the night in a field, they finally reached the last gate at Owthorne with just enough coppers to pay the toll.

In 1848, with George Hunter and R W Dry he formed the Withernsea Primitive Methodist Society. They could not afford to build a chapel and held prayer meetings in their houses. By 1858 the had raised enough money to build a chapel in Alma Street. By this time he was acting as a carrier between Hull and Withernsea, and on his journeys he raised money for a new larger chapel wherever and whenever he could. It has been said that his wife made clothes and crocheted articles which were sold to help the building fund.

In 1879 the present Primitive Methodist Chapel on Hull Road was triumphantly opened. We have been told that Grice Jackson worked energetically both as a carrier and as a preacher for his church until the end of his life in his mid–eighties.

Rodney Smith was born in a gypsy camp at Wanstead on the 31st March 1860. His father Cornelius Smith and his mother Mary Welch were both of gypsy stock. He was one of six children, and his mother died of smallpox when he was still a small boy. At the age of sixteen, whilst walking in the village of Elstow where John Bunyan was born, he decided that he wished to serve God and subsequently converted on the 17th November 1876. He continued to ply his trade as a gypsy hawking from door to door, and often sang hymns to the women in the villages he visited.

As his seventeenth birthday approached, he contacted General Booth of the Salvation Army, informing him that he wished to become a preacher. The outcome was that he left his family and joined the Mission in 1877. It was at this period that he learned to read, and was introduced at meetings as Rodney Smith, the converted gypsy boy. His first Mission in Yorkshire was at Whitby, where he stayed with Elijah Cadman and on his first day addressed six meetings. A young lady who was one of his converts in Whitby, Miss Annie Pennock, daughter of a mercantile mariner, later became his wife on the 17th December 1879. They had two sons and one daughter.

He moved around in the north of England, visiting amongst other places Bolton, Sheffield and Hartlepool. His most successful Mission, however, was in Hull. There were two Mission stations. one at Sculcoates and the other at the Ice House. It was here that he became known as Gypsy Smith. Huge crowds came to every service during his six-month stay in the town, and he claimed that there were two policemen on duty at every meeting.

At this period he began to have doubts about working with the Salvation Army. The issue resolved itself when he was dismissed by General Booth for an alleged breach of the army's rules when he accepted a watch in appreciation of his work by the people of Hanley. Smith continued with his Christian Mission, and in 1883 he was again invited to visit Hull. His welcome was soul stirring: awaiting him at the station was a carriage and a pair of magnificent greys. The enthusiastic throng unharnessed the horses and dragged the carriage themselves on a triumphant tour of the town to enable all to see the celebrated preacher. As previously, huge crowds attended his services every night. Fortunately for the publicans who protested at the fall-off of business, his stay was only for two weeks. Before leaving, he had established a Mission which he entrusted to his sister Mathilda and her husband George Evans.

Gypsy Smith died on board the *Queen Mary* in 1947 on his way to visit America.

Moses Welsby, popularly known as 'Owd Mo', laid the foundation for the use of gospel waggons in Methodism. Owd Mo was born in a public house and at an early age was a confirmed drinker, and like many converts to the faith became almost fanatical in his zealous urge to spread the good word. His first waggon was a caravan which David Pilgrim, a stalwart Methodist, had sparsely furnished and stocked with books. He toured the towns and villages preaching and selling books and Bibles. There were soon numerous vans, such as the one pictured above, which toured all the East Riding. They would be allowed to use a farmer's field or other suitable site, and word would quickly spread giving the proposed time of the meetings. There were usually two evangelists and occasionally a small portable harmonium was incorporated. In the early years of the twentieth century, gospel waggons became part of village life and their visits were eagerly awaited, even if only for the diversion they created in what was usually a predictable way of life of hard work and long hours.

Facing page bottom: Fishing communities had a great respect for Christianity, and many had their own chapel or perhaps a section of a church which was dedicated to the sea and the men who manned the boats. There were dedications to those lost at sea, and as can be seen in the photograph of the Withernsea Fishermen's Chapel, the tools of their trade, the nets, lobster and crab pots, oilskins and pictures of boats.

This picture above shows the study at Roos Rectory during the period from 1900 to 1907 when the vicar was the Rev F R Hawkes Mason. One gains the impression that he was fond of music as his piano is obviously used, and in spite of the numerous ornaments around the room it is exceedingly tidy, with an orderly desk. The flowers in the fireplace add a homely touch.

The Boys' Brigade was founded in Glasgow in 1883 by William Smith (later Sir William). He and two colleagues began the first unit of thirty boys. Sir William remained as secretary until his death in 1914, and the movement grew under his guidance. The Brigade, which spread across the United Kingdom, had a background of religion, its chief aim being to train an individual to become a self-reliant, God-fearing man. Companies were formed by churches and chapels, and took boys at an age when it was hoped that they could be led to membership of the church. There is also a junior movement, the Life Boys.

The Boy Scout movement was founded by Boer War general Sir Robert Baden Powell in 1908. It was expanded rapidly and in 1912 was granted a royal charter. The scout's promise made on his honour was: 'To do his duty to God, and the King, to help other people at all times, and to obey the Scout Law'. A boy could join at the age of eight by becoming a Wolf Cub and become a Scout at the age of eleven, and a Rover Scout at eighteen. As the Scout Law embodied good citizenship, chivalry and skills in outdoor activities, some church elders saw the potential of forming their own Scout troupes, where the boys could be led, like those in the Boys' Brigade, into the ways of Christianity and, hopefully, as adults become full church members.

This scene is typical of many summer events in the East Riding. The tables are set out in the vicarage gardens amid the sunshine. At this particular tea party, the older members of the congregation appear to be seated whilst tea is being served by the younger ladies. The vicarage was often the hub of the social events in a village during the summer, garden parties being a very popular event. In winter the church hall would come into its own for pea and pie suppers, church socials and other similar entertainments. At Christmas, parties were organised for the children, and in some parishes for the poor in all age groups. The ladies would organise bazaars and sales of work to raise funds for such ventures. The sales of work provided a good excuse for social gatherings of ladies all year round as they busily sewed, embroidered and crocheted their contributions for the stalls on sale day.

Some of the ladies of Elstronwick Chapel enjoying a break in their labours as they prepare for their forthcoming bazaar.

This happy group are set to leave for an outing to Withernsea. They are members of the Easington Church Sunday school who are eagerly looking forward to a day of enjoyment. The basket packed with tasty refreshments can be seen at the driver's feet. No doubt there are more. Even the horse will benefit from his day of pleasure, as he will more than likely be left to graze in a field near the town whilst the passengers sample the entertainments offered.

This children's special service took place on Bridlington beach just a few short weeks before the outbreak of the First World War. Similar services were held in summer in resorts all over Britain, the beach being a novel and attractive setting. The Methodists seem to have been particularly adept at stage-managing such events. The ubiquitous entertainments taking place on the beach such as Pierrots, Punch and Judy, and donkey rides drew the children in hordes, and if the service was cleverly timed this audience would join the congregation from the organising church. Children's hymns were sung often the music of a portable harmonium similar to those used by some of the Pierrot troupes. A clever leader of hymn singing could soon have everyone participating, often marrying actions to the tunes, much to the delight of the children, and often their charges. The more serious side would be a short Bible reading or lesson of a moralistic nature, and prayers. In this way, some children who considered Sunday school as 'stuffy' were hopefully relating thoughts of Jesus to more pleasant experiences.

This picture shows the Hull V Salvation Army Band. During the early part of the twentieth century, the bands were part of Sunday in every household. They marched through the streets of their town playing rousing tunes, and at convenient places stopped to hold a short service. They did not confine their activities to their own town but visited nearby units. During the summer, Sunday evenings would always see a Salvation Army band on the promenade or some other strategic spot in the seaside resorts. Many older people speak of this with nostalgia, telling of the feeling of 'belonging' as they joined in the hymn singing with their fellow holidaymakers and friends. When the collecting boxes went round to support their charitable work, most managed to spare a copper or two. The bands were also an integral part of Christmas week in the towns, as they would tour the streets singing carols and adding to the seasonal spirit. This was one of the joys — or annoyances, depending on your attitude — to the often rousing music of Sundays, which has gradually declined since the Second World War.

The War to End all Wars

At the turn of the twentieth century, Britain was at war. The Boer War, with all its attendant patriotic trappings, seemed very far removed from the country as a whole and did not have the same impact on the people as the First World War.

August 1914 was gloriously hot and many families were enjoying holidays at the seaside, which in some cases were to be their last. On the 3rd August, war was declared. This was to prove the most terrible war ever fought. The fighting was no longer the prerogative of the professional soldier, but involved a large proportion of the male population, and a great number of women. Trench warfare was more barbaric than any other military strategy before or since. Casualties mounted at a frightening rate, and those who had forecast peace by Christmas had their complacency shattered. There was not a household in the country left unscathed by this terrible conflict. More men were killed in the trenches than in any other war. The British dead and wounded alone were said to exceed two million, which was more than the estimated numbers for the Second World War. One in ten men under forty-five is said to have been killed and one in five severely wounded. This led to a nation of shocked and bereaved parents, wives and children. There are monuments in almost every town and village in the country erected to the memory of these unselfish and courageous men who went through Hell to their deaths for king and country. The First World War changed the concept of life irrevocably, not only in the physical sense but in a mental and emotional outlook where life was no longer a measured span, but an uncertainty in which one lived almost for the hour.

The city of Hull was particularly affected. It has been claimed that with its many service battalions of the Kitchener Army and its existing regular and Territorial units, Hull sent more men to war than any other city per head of population.

The people of Oppy in France, like those of the East Riding, were an agricultural community, and it was at the infamous Battle of Oppy Wood in May 1917 that the men of Hull and East Yorkshire were slaughtered in their hundreds. Even today families still mourn a father or grandfather who died on that appalling day. Some make a pilgrimage to the monument erected by the people of Oppy in recognition of the men who sacrificed their lives. The inscription reads: 'To the glory of God and in memory of all men of Kingston upon Hull and local units who gave their lives in the First World War 1914–1918. He died to make men Holy. These died to make men free.' In the Battle of the Somme, the East Yorkshire Regiment was awarded two Victoria Crosses.

At home, the civilians in some areas of Yorkshire suffered the Zeppelin raids, and whilst casualties could not conceivably be compared with the ghastly carnage at the front, many people lost not only their homes but their lives, and like the men at the front there was an attitude of living for the present rather than planning for the future.

Rationing was introduced — sugar and flour were in very short supply, butter and even margarine became rare, and man's staple diet, the humble potato, was very difficult to obtain in urban areas. Many of the older generation tell of queuing with their mothers in the hope of obtaining a little bit extra of whatever food they could find.

The concept of work changed dramatically, with women taking on jobs previously done by men only. After an initial attitude of extreme caution, and in some cases rank prejudice by some of the older farmers in the Holderness area, the Land Girls proved themselves more than equal to the job, and were welcomed, especially by those who had encountered hardship in the 1914 harvest, when large numbers of men who had joined the Waggoners Special Reserve — the idea of Sir Mark Sykes of the Sledmere Estate — were immediately mobilised in August 1914. Women in the towns worked on the trams as 'clippies'. There was also work to be found in munitions factories or aircraft factories. This was the first war in which men actually fought in the air. Many women turned to nursing, some saw service at the front, often very close to the action, whilst others worked equally long and hard hours caring for the wounded and disabled who were repatriated to England. They also acquitted themselves well as ambulance drivers. More often than not, these brave women endured appalling conditions and bore with extreme fortitude the grisly and horrifying sights to which they were subjected as a result of the carnage.

This was thought to be the 'war to end all wars' — but sadly, as we are all so painfully aware, this was not to be. In 1939 Britain declared war on Germany. Whilst this had a huge impact on East Yorkshire, particularly the destructive air raids on the city of Hull, we feel that we could not do justice to this conflict and its resulting ramifications in our book.

This pre-war picture taken at Bessingby Camp in 1912 shows soldiers of the Kings Own Yorkshire Light Infantry. There are also boys and civilian men. At this time there was a great interest in the Territorial Army — men liked the idea that they received a few shillings for doing something which they enjoyed. There were weekly drills in a local hall, and in some towns the 'Terriers' had established their own drill halls. The men were eventually put into uniform, and the yearly camp was eagerly awaited, when it was usual to 'go under canvas' with a group of regulars. When war was declared in 1914, many men were at their annual camp, including a group from Bridlington. In some cases they did not even return home but were immediately placed on active service.

Facing page: These lads are a group of recruits or 'Kitchener's Men'. Lord Kitchener put out an appeal for 100,000 volunteers to swell the ranks of the army as the first euphoric rush to enlist eased off. All physically fit men between the ages of nineteen and thirty would be accepted. It was in response to this call that numerous 'Pals Battalions' were raised. These consisted of recruits from one town or city. It is recorded that a street in one Lancashire town lost all its young male residents in one battle.

Hull had four such battalions: the 10th East Yorkshire was the Hull Commercials or 1st Hull Pals; the 11th Yorkshire was the Tradesmans or 2nd Hull Pals; the 12th East Yorkshire was the Sportsmans or 3rd Hull Pals; and the 13th East Yorkshire was the 4th Hull Pals. At least one of the men shown here was a Hull man, as the card was sent to his mother in Hull and refers to a parcel.

Pictured above are two men in charge of an army waggon. It was customary on Wolds farms to use pole waggons like those used by the army. The lads on the farms were skilled in driving these waggons, which were used all year round for the numerous seasonal tasks of the farming calendar. Sir Mark Sykes of Sledmere conceived the idea that it would be a great waste of these special skills if, on the outbreak of hostilities, these men were mobilised and simply dispersed throughout units to serve as riflemen in the trenches, where their vast experience of driving heavily laden waggons across uneven terrain would be lost to the army command. With this in mind, in 1913 he formed the Wolds Waggoners Special Reserve. Each man was given a small payment as a retainer, and in return pledged his services as a driver at home or abroad in the event of war. The members of the Waggoners Special Reserve were mobilised immediately war was declared in August 1914, and were the first civilians to serve overseas.

Facing page: The Waggoners Memorial in Sledmere was built in 1919 of white Portland stone and is twenty feet (6m) in height. It was executed by Mr A Barr who was the mason for Colonel Sir Mark Sykes's Sledmere Estate. The sculptures on the central column were executed by Mr Carlo Magnoni of London to designs drawn up by Sir Mark. They tell the history of the Waggoners Reserve, beginning at the top with the field at Fimber where the annual driving competitions took place; next comes the enrolment of men at Martinmas 1912; the receipt of mobilisation papers and family farewells; embarkation to France; and, at the bottom of the column, examples of German atrocity and a lone Waggoner facing four Germans. There are several verses by Sir Mark Sykes to the glory of these brave men, who were simple, hard-working country men who acquitted themselves with stoic heroism, despite being suddenly thrown into an incomprehensible, bloody and violent war which was none of their doing. Their wives, who were left to cope with the work, appeared to have shared a feeling where pride fought the despair of being able to 'keep things going for him'.

THE MONUMENT SLEDMERE

"I'm Thinking of YOU Every...

At .... —— *A Soldier's Letter.*

I haven't had time to sit down and write,
    And thought perhaps you might grieve :
So I send you this card just to say I'm alright,
    And longing to see you again when on "leave."
When the Empire's Call for more men to fight,
    For her Honour—in me caused a thrill ;
I felt fight I must or else I should "bust,"
    So I'm "Somewhere" in Old England—at drill
The work it is stiff, for we're "at it" all day,
    And sometimes half of the night ;
But we're hardening to it and getting quite fit,
    And thank goodness for "grub" we're alright.
My duty calls me as this picture shows,
    To the Front where the fightin' is done ;
And when *Kitchener's Boys* get their grip on the foe,
    There's no letting go till they've won.
So cheer up, my dear, tho' parted we are,
    And though I'm so far away ;
My loved ones are ever *first* in my thoughts,
    I'm thinking of **YOU** *everyday.*

At "Duty's Call."   *From* .... *(Copyrigh*

This badly distressed postcard was sent to a young woman in Elstronwick from her husband who was one of 'Kitchener's Boys'. It is just another touching example of the jingoism produced under the guise of patriotism by the supporters of Kitchener's policy. In spite of the sentiment of 'don't worry I'm alright' and loving thoughts, it must have been cold comfort for the recipient. Most wives and sweethearts ached for the personal bond of even a short note in the loved one's own hand, which many saw as a renewal of one-to-one contact and took comfort for a while in the confirmation that 'he' was still alive and thinking of them.

Facing page: At 8 am on Wednesday the 16th December 1914, the town of Scarborough was rudely awakened. It was a dark morning with a gloomy mist hanging over the town when the first fusillade of shells from a fleet of six German warships found their target. In defence of this wanton destruction, the Germans described Scarborough — presumably because of its castle — as a fortified town. Three ships, the *Derrflinger, Van der Tann* and *Kolberg,* launched the attack at Scarborough, whilst the other three steamed up the coast to attack Whitby and Hartlepool. In the town of Scarborough, 124 people lost their lives and over 500 were injured. The attack was the subject of indignant protest both at home and abroad. Damage was extensive, affecting all parts of the town, and there are many stories both tragic and of narrow escapes. Our picture shows damage to a house in Wykeham Street where a Mrs Barnett and two children lost their lives.

On the 19th August 1915 the British submarine E13 ran aground on the Danish island of Sathelm whilst on its way to the Baltic. It was shelled by a German torpedo boat, a reprehensible action as the vessel was in neutral waters. Fifteen of the crew were killed. A Danish torpedo boat steamed between the two ships, thus curtailing the attack. Thirteen of the bodies were recovered and taken to Hull on the Danish V/L *Vidar*, being accorded full military honours. The damaged submarine and the rest of the crew were interned, but Lieutenant Commander Layton, who was in command, escaped back to England. Pictured is the procession which took place from Riverside Quay to Paragon Station in Hull, where the *Last Post* was played and a volley of shots was fired. The bodies of the men were sent by rail for burial in their home towns.

Above: This photograph of a motorcyclist was taken by a Paris photographer and sent to a grandmother in Hull from her 'Devoted Grandson'. The date is May 1915 and he has proudly written 'On active service'.

Left: The smart East Yorkshire Regiment soldier from Withernsea clearly shows the uniform of the day. The puttees, which are no longer part of today's army uniform, must have been a problem to new recruits until they acquired the 'knack'.

Even to this day, the word 'Zeppelin' causes some of the older generation to shudder at its mention. This was a new instrument of war, and the means by which the frightened civilian population could be subjected to threat of death raining from above.

When it was realised that attack from the air could become a reality, lighting restrictions were imposed in Hull. Tram windows were dimmed by being treated, and street lamps were painted light blue above a dark blue on the lower part of the glass. When the warning buzzer was heard, all lights had to be extinguished, at the risk of a substantial fine. Several East Riding towns were to suffer attacks, including Beverley, Driffield, Goole, Hedon and Hull.

The first attack on Hull, which proved to be the most serious, came on Sunday the 6th June 1915. The warning was sounded at 10 pm. Apart from people who were injured or killed outright, it has been suggested that a number of people (possibly elderly) died of shock, not only in the Hull raid but in other parts of the country. On that fateful night in Hull, it is recorded that thirteen high-explosive bombs and around fifty incendiary bombs were dropped, killing twenty-four people, seriously injuring another forty, and leaving a trail of devastation through the city. Many were left homeless and bereft, having lost everything they possessed.

Press Bureau, OFFICIAL MESSAGE.
"**A Zeppelin visited the East Coast**
on Sunday night (June 6th, 1915.)
"Incendiary and explosive bombs
were dropped.
"Number of deaths 24; Injured 40."

The Midnight Assassin

A propaganda Zeppelin mourning card recording the deaths of twenty-four people on a raid on the East Coast.

It has been possible to trace details of the man and his ship who wreaked havoc on Hull that night. The Zeppelin was the *Luftschiff 9*, commanded by Kapitan Lieutenant Heinrich Mathy, aged thirty-three. He had previously been a destroyer skipper and spent three years in naval airships. Mathy had a reputation for boldness and determination, and was recognised as a navigational genius. Neither the man nor his ship survived the war. On the 16th September 1916, the *Luftschiff 9* was destroyed by fire in a shed at Fuhlsbuttel. Heinrich Mathy was in command of the ill-fated L31 when it was shot down over Potters Bar by British aircraft on the 9th October 1916. It was recorded that nineteen were believed killed and there were no survivors.

An unexploded Zeppelin incendiary bomb which was dropped on Hull in 1915.

With mobilisation for the First World War, it was completely impossible for the farmers to manage without assistance. Obviously, it was imperative that farming must continue and one of the first concessions was to allow boys to leave school at thirteen to work on the farms. Many country boys took advantage of this and helped on farms for the duration, becoming skilled with horses at an early age, although some lied

about their ages and managed to enlist as young as fifteen and sixteen. In spite of this, more help was still needed, and in 1916 it became obvious that women could provide a useful source of labour. Many country women were already working on farms, but the Women's Land Army gave the opportunity for girls and women to work on the land as an alternative to munitions and other wartime employment. At first the farmers were mostly scornful of the idea that these women, many of them from the towns, could be of any use to them at all. It was claimed that they would 'crack up' under the pressures of early rising and hard work. They reckoned without the determination of these women, many of whom had already suffered bereavement, or lived in the fear for their loved ones. Acceptance of the girls came gradually, but eventually, due to their diverse capabilities, their contribution was acknowledged by all but the most negative thinkers, who still considered that women were only fit for 'house jobs and the hens'.

The photograph shows a young woman from Hull in the uniform of a munitions worker. The uniform was basically a khaki-coloured overall belted at the waist and a hair-confining cap. There were variations: sometimes the caps were of the mob-cap style, sometimes more like the caps worn by cooks in domestic service.

At the outbreak of war, many women and girls went into munitions factories. Like some of the men who enlisted in 1914, a large number lied about their age in order to secure a place. They came from a wide range of backgrounds, and there were more town girls than country girls for the obvious reason that the factories were sited in or around the large urban conurbations. Amongst their numbers were ladies who had worked in shops and offices, and some came from domestic service.

We have been told of a lady who retained her position of lady's maid with a family and also worked in a factory. Due to the paucity of such workers, the employer readily agreed to this, feeling that she would be deemed unpatriotic if she refused her maid's request. The maid was motivated by the high wages which she could save, with marriage in mind when her sweetheart returned. At the same time she had a strong sense of loyalty to her mistress.

Some ladies of leisure who had not previously worked were moved to offer their services, along with many women from less affluent backgrounds. Many of these ladies were genuinely patriotic and felt they were helping their husbands, sweethearts and brothers at the front. Others admitted to less altruistic reasons such as boredom at home. Whatever their reasons, the women worked very hard, often for as long as twelve hours a day, under varying conditions.

Some employers treated the women with the respect they deserved, but others tried to exploit them, offering pitifully low wages for very dangerous jobs. There was not much to be said on the credit side for this type of war work, but on the debit side the least of the disadvantages was the fact that, in some explosive departments, their hair and skin was badly affected, often turning bright yellow. In many cases their health was adversely affected, and some died of a form pernicious anaemia. There was the ever-present threat of an explosion, which caused many women to suffer from what we now recognise as stress-related illness. When such an accident did occur, it was often due to the use of obsolete machinery. Inevitably there were fatalities, and many of these hard-working women were severely maimed.

The East Yorkshire Regiment has a very old tradition. It was raised in 1685 by James II at the time of the Monmouth Rebellion. In 1782 it was listed as 'Yorkshire East Riding', but when regimental titles were reorganised in 1881 it became the East Yorkshire Regiment. In 1935, to mark the silver jubilee of King George V, the title of the Duke of Yorks Own was conferred, as his son, later King George VI, had been colonel-in-chief of the regiment since 1922. The regimental badge is an eight-pointed star with the white rose of York encircled by a laurel wreath with the words East Yorkshire on a scroll at the base.

In 1914, Hull formed a special battalion of the East Yorkshire Regiment. These were recruited men and were called the Hull Commercials. After a period of service in Egypt, they were moved to France to the Somme in readiness for the 'Big Push'. Before the attack began, there were more than one million men camped on the downs of Picardy, including the Hull men. On the first day the British suffered more than 60,000 casualties. The Commercials lost more than 100 men from their total of 600 on the 1st July 1916. In May 1917 they were further devastated at Oppy Wood, as described in the beginning of this chapter. The picture shows some of the brave men of the East Yorkshire Regiment in camp. It would be interesting to know how many of the men in the picture survived the war.

The picture was taken at Rugely Camp in April 1917. The Battle of Arras began in that month, and on the 1st May some of the Hull Brigade were preparing to take part in the battle and marched to positions in trenches near Oppy Wood. It is recorded that 209 men from the Hull battalions were killed in a few short hours on the day of the battle at Oppy Wood, about half of whom had been enlisted in that seaport. By this time, most of the men who had originally enlisted were weary of war and grossly disillusioned by the jingoistic rhetoric of their leaders in an attempt to salve the conscience of society. Despite this, they did their duty without question. Did any of these young men who appear in our photograph fight at Arras? If so, did they live to fight another day on some other field of carnage?

A poignant reminder of the men from Manchester Street in Hull who laid down their lives for their King and Country in the 'War to End all Wars'. Pictures of some of the men are incorporated in a tasteful arrangement of flowers. The frame in the middle is a roll of honour with the names of the dead inscribed. There are items of remembrance for those who lost their lives at sea, and there were many of those from Hull. This is not an isolated example of such a memorial — many areas produced similar tributes.

Select Bibliography

Chapman, M and B, *Pierrots of the Yorkshire Coast* (1988).

Chapman, B and M, *Kingston upon Hull* (1996).

Chapman, B and M, *Holderness in Old Picture Postcards* (1995).

Chapman, M and B, *Withernsea* (1996).

Chapman, B and M, *Around Goole* (1997).

Chapman, B and M, *Beverley in Old Picture Postcards* (1997).

Easdown, M, *Piers of Disaster* (1996).

Fisher, K, *Hollym* (1990).

Howard, A, *York* (1995).

Markham, J, *Hunting Scenes — Holderness Hunt* (1989).

Percy, J, *Scarborough in the 50s and 60s* (1994).

Smith, M H, *Hornsea a Century Ago* (1993).

Southwell, G L, *Hornsea* (1995).

Southwell, G L, *Hornsea in Old Picture Postcards* (1993).

Young, M, *Selby* (1995).

Whittaker, J, *Old Withernsea Remembered* (1990).

Index of Places

Index of People